The Joy of
Feeling
Good

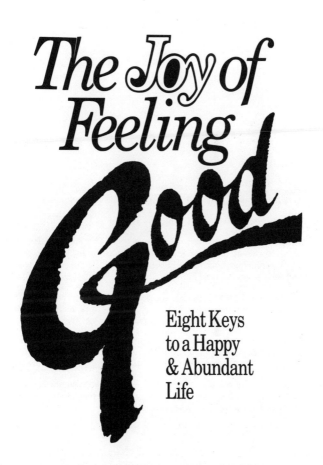

The Joy of Feeling Good

Eight Keys
to a Happy
& Abundant
Life

WILLIAM A. MILLER

AUGSBURG Publishing House • Minneapolis

THE JOY OF FEELING GOOD
Eight Keys to a Happy and Abundant Life

Scripture quotations unless otherwise noted are from the Holy Bible: New International Version. Copyright 1978 by the New York International Bible Society. Used by permission of Zondervan Bible Publishers.

Scripture quotations marked NEB are from The New English Bible. Copyright The Delegates of the Oxford University Press and The Syndics of the Cambridge University Press, 1961, 1970. Reprinted by permission.

Unless otherwise noted, the names of persons whose stories are told in this book are fictitious, and the specific details of their stories have been altered so as to make them unrecognizable.

The story of the Rev. Peter Niewiek is gratefully used by permission of Peter Niewiek.

Library of Congress Cataloging-in-Publication Data

Miller, William A., 1931–
  THE JOY OF FEELING GOOD.

  1. Happiness.   2. Contentment.   I. Title.
BF575.H27M53   1986   158'.1   86-20574
ISBN 0-8066-2236-9

Manufactured in the U.S.A.   APH 10-3601

         3   4   5   6   7   8   9   0   1   2   3   4   5   6   7   8   9

Other books by William A. Miller

To
my family

Marilyn
Eric
Mark and Dana

Contents

The Joy
of Feeling Good

Why do you suppose some people always seem to be feeling good? You know the ones I mean—you ask Sam, "How are you doing?" and Sam replies, "Fine, thanks." You know he's sincere and not simply muttering an appropriate response to your greeting, because you've known Sam for years and that's the way he appears most of the time. Sure, there have been days when he has said, "Oh, not so good today. I think I need to give my hobbies more time," or "Well, I've been better. I need to quit trying to live my brother-in-law's life for him." But by and large, Sam seems to be feeling good about himself and about life.

These "Sams" are good-natured and healthy; they appear to be happy, satisfied, and relatively fulfilled. Most of them are ambitious and seem to do well at what they do. Many of them are people of faith, hopeful types who are more optimistic than pessimistic.

They laugh a lot and don't seem to take life or themselves too seriously. But they're responsible people; you can count on them. You know where they stand, because they will tell you.

It doesn't seem to make any difference whether these people have money or don't, whether they're highly educated or not, what kind of house they live in, what church they belong to, or what kind of work they do. They are people like you and me. But they seem to have something special, something "more."

Sam and others like him know the joy of feeling good. Feeling good involves your mood, attitude, how you view yourself, your feelings, how honest you are with yourself, the condition of your faith, and your social relationships. The joy of feeling good comes from being emotionally, spiritually, and socially sound.

We need to rediscover some of the very basic principles of living that people like Sam have retained and put into practice. People like Sam simply live out in their lives many of the common-sense principles that probably are familiar to all of us.

The purpose of this book is to bring to light what Sam and people like him practice daily, and to help you do the same, so that you, too, may know the joy of feeling good.

Feeling good starts on the inside, with a way of thinking, a way of believing, and a way of acting. For more than 25 years I have counseled with people in their movement toward happier and more satisfying lives. Over those years I have discovered that human beings have *several prime needs*. When these needs are appropriately met, we experience the joy of feeling good. Some of these needs are:

(1) to be proud of ourselves, respect ourselves, and love ourselves as God loves us.

(2) to know what we stand for, what we believe in, and what we value.

(3) to care about others, love them, and invest ourselves in them.

(4) to know and understand ourselves as best we can, to accept even what is unlovely about ourselves.

(5) to strive toward faithfully using our talents and abilities, to reach for the capability God has given us.

(6) to risk expressing even our deepest feelings, to share in intimacy, and to enjoy spontaneity.

(7) to be rooted in a source of existence that is outside ourselves, to feel an immovable foundation that will support us throughout our existence, and to worship a loving, giving God.

(8) to be our own man or woman, to take responsibility for our lives, and to live our days in confidence.

Based on these eight needs, I have developed eight keys to a happy and abundant life. Each chapter in this book presents one of the keys and shows how you can use it to unlock the secrets of feeling good.

Putting these keys into practice is no easy task. Most of us have developed habits and attitudes that work against us, and these may be difficult to modify.

One of the basic principles that runs through all eight keys is the need for *balance*. As life presents us with challenges and choices, the best course is usually to find a healthy, middle path between two extremes.

For example, Key Number 1 involves finding your path between feeling as if you are a worthless person and feeling arrogant. Most of us get into trouble when we allow ourselves to move too far to the left or to the right on the "line" or "continuum" between the two extremes. In the case of Key Number 1, I have found that Christians are more prone to feelings of worthlessness than they are to feelings of arrogance.

In the pages that follow, occasionally a suggestion that is offered to achieve balance may call for behavior that feels wrong or inappropriate. Don't be alarmed. For example, if you find it easy to let others take advantage of you, the act of asserting your own legitimate needs and concerns does not necessarily make you arrogant! It may merely bring you to a healthy midpoint between the two extremes. You may only subjectively *feel* as if you are acting in an arrogant way.

My wife Marilyn had a terrible time taking tennis lessons after having played for years without benefit of professional advice. What the pro told her to do felt radically wrong, and unlearning what she had believed was correct seemed absurd. Nevertheless, she persevered, and today she plays well.

The rewards that come from mastering the eight keys to a happy and abundant life far outweigh the effort needed to shift attitudes, alter habits, and change behavior. And beyond that, there is the tremendous joy that comes when we can genuinely feel good about ourselves, about others, and about life.

Eight Keys to a Happy and Abundant Life

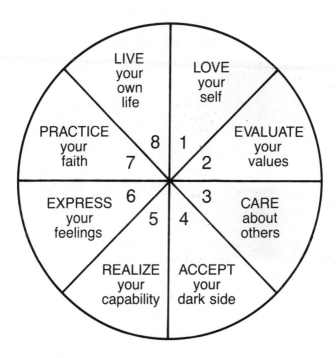

1. *Love your self* and find your own place between a feeling of worthlessness at one extreme on the continuum and a philosophy of arrogance at the other.

Worthlessness   **Arrogance**

2. *Evaluate your values* and find your own place between an attitude of "anything goes" at one extreme on the continuum and a philosophy that says, "Everything is black or white" at the other.

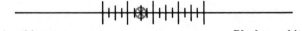

Anything goes   **Black or white**

3. *Care about others* and find your path between an attitude of self-sacrifice at one extreme on the continuum and a position of self-centeredness at the other.

Self-sacrifice   **Self-centeredness**

4. *Accept your dark side* and find your path between seeing yourself as an angel at one extreme on the continuum and as a devil at the other.

Angel   **Devil**

5. *Realize your capability* and find your path between a position of sloth at one extreme on the continuum and a posture of workaholism at the other.

Sloth   **Workaholism**

6. *Express your feelings* and find your path between an attitude of suppression at one extreme on the

continuum and a position of impulsiveness at the other.

Suppression   **Impulsiveness**

7. *Practice your faith* and find your path between a philosophy of overdependence at one extreme on the continuum and an attitude of independence at the other.

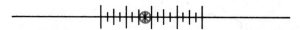

Overdependence   **Independence**

8. *Live your own life* and find your path between an attitude of powerlessness at one extreme on the continuum and a position of omnipotence at the other.

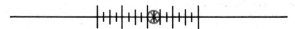

Powerlessness   **Omnipotence**

Key Number 1

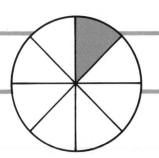

Love Your Self

Finding your path between worthlessness and arrogance.

*I*t's a great feeling to be able to look into the mirror and like the person you see. I see my reflection and I feel good about myself because I know I am a person of worth and value. Oh yes, I know I have my faults and weaknesses, but I also have abilities and strengths. I thank God for being me. I like me."

We were near the end of our hour together. I had never heard Jeanne speak so clearly about the transformation that she had helped to bring about in her life. I was pleased to hear her say what she did, but I was not surprised. For I had walked with her along a journey out of the shadows of a sense of worthlessness into the bright sunlight of being able to love herself.

Jeanne's story is not unique. Hundreds of thousands of us have experienced it in one form or another. The home setting in which Jeanne grew up did not allow for her to develop a healthy image of herself. Her

mother and father certainly fulfilled parental obligations, but they failed to go beyond that to help instill
in Jeanne a "comfortableness" with herself and a
gentle pride in herself. Instead they consistently reminded her of her failures and shortcomings; how she
could do better, no matter how well she had done; that
other girls did such-and-such and why couldn't she.
They never put their arm around her shoulder, smiled
warmly into her face, and said quietly, "You're OK,
kid; you're alright—and I love you."

As time passed, Jeanne's image of herself slipped
lower and lower, because she focused on what was
"wrong" with herself and failed to see and take into
account her strengths, abilities, and achievements. She
discounted her successes and magnified her failures.
She put herself into relationships where her poor image
of herself would be reinforced by people who gave her
the same message her parents had given her. For
Jeanne, life became little more than an experience of
depression, dissatisfaction, and unhappiness.

In the times we spent together Jeanne struggled to
lay aside her image of a worthless self, to accept herself
as she was, to see her positive qualities as well as the
negative ones, and to love herself the way she intellectually knew that God loved her. She found it difficult to admit that she was mistaken in continuing to
believe her parents' evaluation of her—that she could
never do anything "right." But her dissatisfaction provided sufficient motivation and energy for her to remain in her journey toward a healthy self-image. We
celebrated her successes along the way and groaned
over her backsliding into old, self-defeating behaviors.

Ultimately her persistence paid off. Jeanne does not
live in the fantasy that her life is perfect and fully

satisfying, but now she knows that life can also be beautiful.

Life *can* be beautiful when you love yourself. There is a deep sense of well-being in the ability to smile lovingly at yourself and feel the joy of being you. How much better you feel when the image you see in the mirror evokes self-love rather than self-hate!

Your Self-Image

People have a wide range of self-images—all the way from a despondent sense of worthlessness to the extreme of blatant arrogance, with a myriad of grades in between. An extreme focusing on *worthlessness* includes self-effacement and self-hate: "I don't like myself"; "I can't stand myself"; "I'm not good for anything"; "I'll never amount to anything"; "I can't do anything right"; "I'm a zero"; "I'm the worst." I accuse, convict, and condemn myself.

An extreme focusing on *arrogance* includes haughtiness, big-headedness, and vanity; being pompous, contemptuous, insolent, domineering, stiff-necked; appearing as superior, condescending, presumptuous, overbearing, and snobbish. "I am the epitome of greatness—the acme, the zenith, the apex." The universe orbits around me.

These extremes seem worlds apart. Yet often those who appear at the extreme of arrogance are similar to those at the extreme of worthlessness, because their true image of themselves is actually quite poor. Arrogance often proves to be an overcompensation for a poor self-image; it serves as a cover-up, a facade designed to hide the poor self-image underneath.

Both the extremes of worthlessness and arrogance are dangerous because of their destructive potential. A sense of worthlessness can cripple and paralyze a person. One feels deeply despondent, with little motivation even to live. Blatant arrogance provokes others to attack or reject and places the person in severe jeopardy.

We experience the joy of feeling good when we are able to achieve an image of self that is somewhere between these two extremes. Our individual balance points will certainly vary from person to person, with some being more toward one end of the continuum and others toward the other. Our balance points will also vary within ourselves from time to time. At some times we may feel closer to one end of the continuum, and at other times closer to the other end.

This is also true of the other keys described in this book. We simply are not carbon copies of each other. Nor are we static beings. But feeling good comes from avoiding extremes and finding a balance point between them by bringing the two opposites together.

What Is It Like to Love Yourself?

What is it like to love yourself? Why is it good and desirable? Here are 12 attributes of those who have a healthy self-image and love themselves.

(1) People who have a healthy self-image and love themselves feel good about themselves. When Jeanne looked in her mirror and saw her reflection, she didn't feel disgust; she didn't look at the image and say, "You make me sick." She felt pleased about herself and comfortable with herself. A healthy self-image gives

you a sense of security and a reasonable self-confidence.

(2) People who have a healthy self-image and love themselves accept themselves not only in their strengths but in their weaknesses as well. Perfection is impossible for us human beings. If we go after it we deny our humanity and reject ourselves. When we love ourselves it is not possible to attempt perfection. We accept our failures, shortcomings, faux pas, mistakes, and misjudgments, as well as the truth of the statement, "I cannot do all things." To love myself is to know my limitations (mostly from experience) and to accept them. To love myself is to know my strengths (mostly from experience) and to celebrate them.

(3) People who have a healthy self-image and love themselves believe God loves them and cares about them. Most people who love themselves also believe God loves them. This is in fact the foundation of their ability to love themselves. They love God and they love themselves because God has first loved them. They believe that the Bible reveals God as a loving parent who cares about them like precious children. There is respect for God but not fear; love casts out fear. Those who love themselves feel the support, strength, and presence of God in their lives.

(4) People who have a healthy self-image and love themselves believe they are doing what God wants them to do in loving themselves. It's not unusual to hear someone say, "Love myself? Isn't that selfish and wrong?" People who love themselves do so at God's command: "Love your neighbor as yourself"

(Matt. 22:39). People must love themselves before they are able to love anyone else.

(5) People who have a healthy self-image and love themselves expect positive experiences from life. People who love themselves also expect others to accept them. Those who have a self-image of worthlessness expect others to reject them, put them down, or at best, tolerate them. Those who have a self-image of arrogance expect to dominate others ("Get them before they get me"), to let them know who they're dealing with.

There is a sense of well-being in being able to meet other people as peers and to expect that these encounters will be positive experiences. Of course not *all* encounters will provide positive experiences. But people who love themselves do not enter the encounters of life expecting rejection or looking for a fight.

(6) People who have a healthy self-image and love themselves feel no need to fall ill. There is evidence to indicate that people with low self-esteem and poor self-image may unconsciously become ill in order to receive the attention, love, and affection they desperately crave but feel unworthy to ask for or receive. In health these people may crave love and care, but they neither receive it voluntarily nor ask for it. In illness, however, they will receive it in a sanctioned way from relatives, possibly from friends and medical personnel.

People who have a healthy self-image and love themselves receive affection, attention, and love from others through everyday living. They project a positive attitude, and others usually respond to them. There is therefore no need to unconsciously "stage" an illness in order to get attention, care, and affection.

(7) People who have a healthy self-image and love themselves graciously accept compliments without feeling embarrassed. This is a hallmark of positive self-image and healthy self-love. Those with poor self-image do not know what to do with compliments or praise. Usually they are embarrassed by the experience, and in an attempt to escape, they reject or greatly discount the compliment.

People who love themselves accept positive feedback with grace. "Thank you very much. I'm pleased that you liked my performance." "I'm glad that what I had to say helped you in some way." People with a healthy self-image quietly store away in their treasure box of memories these positive strokes, warm fuzzies, and reinforcers. They become reminders of good experiences and help raise their spirits when their self-image slides down a bit. There is no need to boast or brag, not even to themselves. They simply thank the giver and treasure the gift.

(8) People who have a healthy self-image and love themselves have reasonable pride in themselves and feel good about their accomplishments. True humility is to be able to applaud yourself inwardly just as readily as you would applaud another person outwardly for accomplishing the same thing. People who love themselves know their talents and abilities just as well as they know their shortcomings and weaknesses. They have a quiet pride in their achievements and can celebrate when they constructively use the talents God gave them. They know that to refuse to be proud of themselves jeopardizes their ability to be proud of others. When we are able to rejoice in our own accomplishments, we feel free to praise others for their achievements as well.

Simply observing a game of football reinforces this observation. Notice how players celebrate their accomplishments on the field and how easily they celebrate their teammates' accomplishments. Incidentally, have you ever seen a receiver catch a 40-yard pass in the end zone for a touchdown, then casually toss the ball over his shoulder saying, "Oh, it was nothing"?

(9) People who have a healthy self-image and love themselves feel no need to impress others or flaunt themselves. Those who consistently remind us of how great they are cause us to wonder how great they really are. People who love themselves quietly go about their business without calling attention to who they are or what they have accomplished. They have no need to put on airs, puff up, or pull rank. Their self-confidence is authentic and does not need reinforcement by an arrogant stance. Those whose image of themselves is shaky and whose self-confidence is at least uncertain frequently appear arrogant in an effort to keep other people from getting too close. They fear that others might discover their shakiness and uncertainty and spoil their image of being on top of things.

(10) People who have a healthy self-image and love themselves make loving spouses. Positive self-regard is an absolute necessity if one is to love another person. A very common issue in unfortunate marriage matches occurs when a person with a poor self-image marries a person with a healthy self-image, with the hope of enhancing his or her image through intimate contact, osmosis, or heaven-only-knows how. This does not happen, because the spouse with a healthy self-image faces the formidable task of trying to love a person who does not love him or herself. Very often

the spouse with a healthy self-image gives up, saying, "How can I love you when you don't even love yourself?"

Persons who will not love themselves cannot authentically love others. They can substitute adoration, servanthood, or worship, but authentic love will not occur until they come to truly love themselves. This is why we hear such romantic phrases as, "I worship the ground you walk on," "I adore you," or "I will be your slave forever." Such statements speak mostly of infatuation and often indicate an absence of authentic love.

Occasionally in a marriage relationship one spouse will suffer a severe loss of self-love and positive self-image. Perhaps because of loss of job, betrayal by a friend or colleague, or a major failure, one spouse falls into self-disgust and self-effacement. The other spouse then has a difficult time continuing to love him or her. The "fallen" spouse feels unworthy of being loved and must regain a positive self-image and self-love before the marriage relationship can be restored to one of love and respect. Counseling that "treats" only the dynamics of the loss (firing, betrayal, failure) and fails to deal with the person's self-image will be unsuccessful in helping the couple through the crisis and toward restoration.

But couples who *do* have healthy self-images and who love themselves as individuals come together into a relationship of mutual love and respect. Self-acceptance allows them to accept each other without the need to make them over into their own image. There is support of one another, celebration of one another's strengths, and an effort to help each other with their weaknesses.

(11) People who have a healthy self-image and love themselves make loving parents. The factor that seems to be most important in shaping a person's self-image is the influence of home and family. Mostly unwittingly, parents shape their children's self-image virtually every day of their growing-up years. Therefore parents who love themselves and talk about the importance of positive self-images may in a natural way offer their children a midpoint—a balance point—between the extremes of worthlessness and arrogance. Such parents demonstrate the wholesomeness of self-love and self-acceptance and avoid instilling feelings of shame or guilt in their children. They demonstrate love, caring, and positive concern for people of all sorts and thus help their children avoid the extreme of arrogance, snobbishness, and disregard for others.

(12) People who have a healthy self-image and love themselves are able to do well with Key Number 3. Key Number 3 is, "Care about others." If I am critical of myself and heap shame or guilt on myself for my failures and weaknesses, I will not be able to accept the failures and weaknesses of anyone else. I may consciously *say,* "It's OK for you," but my unconscious (which convicts me for my weakness) will not let you go scot free in your failures and weaknesses. In some way my nonacceptance of your imperfection will find an expression—perhaps overtly, but more often covertly.

A close relative of mine posed a real mystery to me in my growing up years. She was a churchly woman and presented an imposing public presence of charity and love. Privately, however, she verbalized deep prejudices and strong resentments toward many individuals. It wasn't until many years later, long past the innocence of youth, that I realized the dynamic that was at work in her. She had come to seriously dislike herself and had become a bitter person. She would not love herself, and consequently she could not love anyone else. She continued to go through the motions and say the right words, but her regard for others was hollow, only a public appearance.

Four Obstacles to Avoid

How then should one proceed to develop the state of mind that marks healthy self-love and a positive self-image? There are several suggestions I have to offer that have emerged out of my years of working with others. But before we begin it is helpful to call attention to four pitfalls that need to be avoided on this journey.

(1) Hearing old messages that you should not love yourself. Hearing old messages that you should not love yourself or that it is wrong to have "too high" an image of yourself can present a formidable obstacle. Memories of growing up at home are very vivid to most of us. "As far back as I can remember," Harry said, "I could never do anything right for my dad. When he would tell me to do something he would invariably end the instruction by saying, 'And for heaven's sake, don't screw it up.' Most of the time he would watch me or at least keep checking on me while I was doing the task. This made me awfully nervous and I guess sort of set me up to screw up.

"I learned to read his signals," continued Harry. "When he was scrutinizing my work he would let out sighs. These were indications that I had just done something that he thought I should not have done. When the sighs got pretty close together I knew the end was at hand. He would lose it, and harshly say to me, 'O here, let me do it. I should have done it myself in the first place. You can't do anything right.'

"I remember the time he said, 'Let's build a model airplane.' The implication was that we would build it together. But I couldn't see how that was possible. And I was right. He gave me the task of constructing the wing because he said that was easier than building the fuselage. Everything went OK for a while—until I cut one of the balsa strips too short and he said, 'Now look what you've done; you've ruined that piece of wood. They don't give you enough pieces in the kit to keep ruining them. You better let me do this or we won't have any airplane at all.'

"In time he finished the airplane (it was a glider) and he said, 'Let's take 'er out and see how she sails.' I was afraid to even hold the thing for fear it would disintegrate in my hand and he would 'kill' me. But we went up on a small hill close to home and he showed me how to hold the glider, cock my wrist, pull my arm back, thrust it forward (ever so slightly upward) and let 'er fly.

"My hand was sweating and I was silently praying, 'O dear God, please let it fly.' I followed his instructions and thrust the thing forward. But I guess I must have held onto it a little too long because it angled down from my launch height and hit the ground, nose first, about six feet in front of me.

"I thought he would have a stroke," Harry said. "He flailed his arms in the air and shouted at me, 'What in the name of God is the *matter* with you? Look what you've gone and done now.' Actually the damage to the airplane was minimal; but that was of little significance. That event turned out to be both the beginning and the end of my glider flying."

No doubt the damage to the glider *was* minimal; but the damage to Harry's self-image was substantial. "How can I love myself when I can't do anything right, when I'm all thumbs, when whatever I touch turns into a mess? He's right; there must be something the matter with me. I'll never amount to anything."

No doubt Harry's father had no awareness of what he was doing to his son's self-image. After all, he didn't sit down and plot out how to transform his son's self-image into self-hate and a sense of worthlessness. But because Harry's father's image of *himself* was so poor and because he refused to accept the normal short-comings of his son, that was precisely what he did.

Stories like Harry's are legion. Tom told me how as a young man he would come down the stairs in the morning, feeling good about himself and the world in general, go into the kitchen, and say cheerily to his mother, "Good morning." Whereupon she would turn around, purse her lips, and then say slowly and sternly, "Just . . . wait."

Those two words were enough to fully convince any young, developing person to expect the worst: "So you think it's a good morning, eh? Well let me tell you something. Wipe that silly smile off your face and get realistic. Life is not what it appears to be. A good morning, eh? Well just you wait—you'll see. God knows what tragedy is right around the corner. Etc., etc., etc."

Some parents refuse to support their children in their efforts or compliment their achievements: "I don't want you to grow up to have a big head. People don't like people who have big heads." Or parents may downplay their children's accomplishments: "Hmpf! That's not bad; but you could have done it better if you'd spent less time listening to that crazy music."

Old messages die hard because they were planted early and have deep roots. Furthermore, to suggest that my parents were wrong in what they told me about myself may smack of disrespect, so I may be reluctant to believe it.

(2) The influence of society in general and sometimes of religious people in particular. The parent who tells a child, "People don't like people who have big heads," is simply reflecting part of our culture. We think that to compliment, give positive feedback, and encourage self-love and a healthy self-image will push people into a state of egomania and they will act like they have "big heads."

When I was 13 years old, I sketched a pretty good picture of a horse's head. I was quite proud of my drawing, and I showed it to my stepmother. She admitted that it wasn't bad. When my stepfather came home from work I hurried to show my drawing to him. "Not bad for a 13-year-old, eh?" I said to him. Whereupon my stepmother announced, "I guess we'll have to widen all the doorways in the house now, so Bill can get his big head through."

Arrogance, of course, is a sin. It destroys relationships and injures people. Little wonder that society in general and Christians in particular should want to guard against it. But in our attempt to avoid fostering arrogance, we have gone to the other extreme of fostering a poor self-image or even a sense of worthlessness.

There is a natural tendency within most of us to compliment, congratulate, and applaud the talents and actions of others. That, of course, makes the recipient vulnerable to arrogance. So to deal with this, society invented false humility. False humility is designed to receive positive feedback and defuse it by heavily discounting it or completely rejecting it.

Let's say I have practiced diligently a piece on the piano. After I have performed the piece well you say, "Bill, that was great! You did a marvelous job." To avoid the dangers of accepting this compliment I would either heavily discount it ("Oh, I should have played with more vigor") or reject it ("Oh, it was nothing"). Either way, my response is a lie.

Nevertheless, such behavior is reinforced by society (I will be considered a humble person, modest, unassuming), and so I will be encouraged to continue it.

If we believe that our talents and abilities are truly gifts from God with which God has blessed us, what kind of statement do we make when we say, "It was nothing"? Not only is my statement a lie, it is also a slap in God's face.

(3) The payoffs for projecting a poor self-image. While we can build an excellent case for loving oneself and possessing a good, healthy self-image, there is still something enticing about a poor self-image.

It is possible to avoid considerable responsibility by having a poor self-image. You can sit on the sidelines of life and avoid involvement. "Oh, I can't do that," and "I would never be able to do that," can protect a person from carrying many normal responsibilities.

(4) The power of expectation. Self-doubts are real, no matter what a person's self-image is. Even the person with true self-love and a healthy, positive self-image experiences self-doubts, so those who are moving toward this will experience them also.

When David was laid off from his middle management position it was a terrible blow to his self-image. So much of himself was tied up in what he did that he experienced a deep personal loss when he lost his job. However, he immediately went out into the marketplace to find a new position.

His first job interview went poorly. He had not interviewed for a job for years and he "froze" at some of the interviewer's questions. He thought his next interview went somewhat better, but he still came off poorly and felt rejected. As he opened the door to his third interview he said to himself, "I guess I'll blow this one too." Sure enough, his prediction was accurate.

Often we unconsciously manipulate the environment to fulfill expectations. Grace told me how she had "inadvertently" cut her hand opening a can of beans. It wasn't a severe cut and it would not have been significant except for the circumstances. She had been to her mother's home for a visit and discovered that the kitchen sink drain was clogged shut. Knowing that Grace was handy around the house, her mother asked her if she would fix it. Grace went to work and in short order got the water flowing easily down the drain again. Both her mother and her sister complimented her on her skill and her good work. However, all this positive feedback was too much for Grace. She left her mother's home thinking, "Something's bound to happen to shoot down this good stuff." Sure enough, when she got home and began to prepare dinner she cut her hand opening the can. Then she was able to say, "I knew it. I knew something would happen."

Grace had been working to move out of her poor self-image to a healthier one. It was a struggle for her, as it is for most of us. She had come to the point of understanding the dynamics that were at play in her experience, and she could rightly analyze what had taken place. "I got all these positive strokes from my mother and sister and I must have said to myself, 'That doesn't fit Grace as I know her.' I knew something had to happen to wipe that out. So when I got home I cut myself to prove that I really am a klutz and not a capable person."

Each one of these four obstacles needs to be recognized as one moves toward a healthy sense of self-love. But it can be self-defeating to focus on them. It is much more effective to concentrate on the positive steps that can be taken.

Twelve Steps to a Healthy Self-Love and a Positive Self-Image

(1) Employ the power of positive expectation. We have just seen illustrations of the power of negative expectations—how people can succeed in reinforcing a poor self-image. *The power of positive expectation is even stronger.* If we recognize the attractiveness of a positive self-image and decide that it is what we truly desire, we will be highly motivated to move toward that goal. If that is what you really want, then believe

that you can achieve it and you will set yourself up to do so. You can do it!

(2) Listen to the Word. Both the Old and the New Testaments speak clearly of our worth and value and the need for us to love ourselves. The psalmist said that God has created us with dignity and has crowned us with glory and honor (Psalm 8). Jesus referred to us as "the light of the world" and "the salt of the earth" (Matt. 5:13-14). This is a very special description because in Jesus' day, light and salt were highly valuable commodities. Both the Hebraic Law (Lev. 19:18) and Jesus' reiteration of it (Matt. 22:39) assume that we should love ourselves. Our worth and value were clearly expressed by the apostle Paul: "You see, at just the right time, when we were still powerless, Christ died for the ungodly. Very rarely will anyone die for a righteous man, though for a good man someone might possibly dare to die. But God demonstrates his own love for us in this: While we were still sinners, Christ died for us" (Rom. 5:6-8).

(3) Believe what you hear in the Word. What the Bible says about the worth and value of human beings applies to *all* human beings. What the Bible says about loving oneself applies to all of us. It will do no good to say, "Oh yes, I hear and I know. And that's wonderful for *other* people, but it's not for me." Believe what you know is the truth. Take it into your own heart and your own life. It is *not* too good to be true. It *is* true. *This is the foundation of feeling good*—to know that you are a creation of almighty God, a creation of great worth and value. Love that creation. Love your self!

(4) Develop your track record and salute it. Go to a store and purchase a spiral notebook. Set aside at least three hours of time. Go back as far as you can recall and write in the notebook *all* the good, positive, kind, charitable things you have done, words you have said, and gifts you have given. Start at the earliest time you can recall and work your way up to the present. Record them *all,* no matter how insignificant they may seem. Those are the ones that add up. Most of us accomplish only a few "biggies" in our lifetime. Review this list with the thought in mind to celebrate your accomplishments. This is an arduous assignment, but those who have completed it have told me how worthwhile it was. It helped them to begin focusing at least as much on the positives in their life as on the negatives.

(5) Become your own evaluator. Suggestion number four is only the beginning. Continue keeping a daily log of your positives: achievements, accomplishments, kindnesses. Let yourself become your own evaluator. Believe that your worth is intrinsic and is *not dependent on others' evaluations of you.* Many of us consistently look to others for an evaluation of ourselves. Certainly their evaluation is important and can be helpful. However, as you move toward greater self-love and a healthier self-image, the more you will become your own evaluator.

Incidentally, if you ever begin to think that keeping your track record in that spiral notebook is too much work, remember this story. A woman named Lucy, who had struggled with a poor self-image for most of her life, completed her notebook and kept it up daily. But in the process of moving toward a healthy self-image the obstacles became too much for her and she quit trying. A long period of time passed as Lucy became more despondent and her self-hatred grew. One evening, in the midst of despair, she prepared to take her own life. But for some reason it occurred to her to look once again at her notebook of achievements. It had been a long time since it had been opened and it was almost as if this was the first time she had read the words that she had written. She became engrossed in the positive things she read about herself and found new courage. The cheap spiral notebook that listed her record of achievements saved her life!

(6) Separate who you are from what you do. In our society people have become increasingly identified with what they do. When introduced to someone at a party, the first thing most of us do is ask, "What do you do?" "Where do you work?" It is as if we had no identity without our work. Our worth and value seem to be directly related to our productivity. If our productivity is cut off because of injury, illness, or a layoff, our self-image takes a beating.

On your journey toward greater self-love and a healthy self-image, remember that you have worth and value because you are a creation of God, not because you are a productive employee or a full-time homemaker. Do not allow your self-love and self-image to become totally wrapped up in what you do.

(7) Leave old messages behind and move on. Set some time aside, take a pad of paper, sit down, and write out all the old messages that inhibit you or prohibit you from loving yourself and enjoying a healthy self-image; messages such as, "You'll never amount

to anything," "Can't you do better than that?" "Don't think too highly of yourself," "You think you're too good for us, don't you?" etc., etc. Leave some space in front of each message so that when you have completed your list you can go back and write in, as best you can recall, where the message came from: dad, mom, grandparents, teachers, pastor, read it in a book, heard it in church, etc. You probably won't be able to recall where all the messages came from, but don't be concerned; you'll remember enough.

As you realize that you no longer believe those messages, take them one by one and admit to yourself that you made a mistake—that you were wrong ever to believe them. Don't make excuses; simply admit your mistake, give thanks to God for realizing that you *were* mistaken, and announce to yourself that there is no need any longer to remain in your mistake and believe the messages. Yes, you believed them *then,* but now you know better and you don't have to believe them anymore.

So far this process will not have dealt with the feelings that were also generated along the way. So it is necessary to sit down with a trusted friend or professional who will keep your confidence, and there express openly the anger, grief, disappointment, and hurt—all the feelings that rose up within you when you realized what had been done to you and how it has affected your life and your self-image.

It is important to forgive the people who implanted these messages, and in your heart to accept them where they are. You do not have to agree with them in order to be able to accept them. All that is necessary is to accept them as they are, with all their flaws. Then you will be free. When the old messages begin to sound their disapproval of what you are about, blow the whistle at their first utterance, dismiss them, and move on.

(8) Examine and critique your negative thoughts. Most of us can get into faulty thinking patterns without much difficulty. We can overgeneralize and extrapolate a lifetime experience from one or two events: after a romantic breakup it's easy to say, "I'm unlovable; no one will ever have me." We can jump to conclusions, making assumptions that may be light years from the truth. A colleague passes me in the hall, reading a document as he walks. I say, "Good morning." He passes by without even raising his head. I tell myself, "I must have done something to offend him. What could I have done?" We can get into all-or-nothing thinking.

Do not settle for negative conclusions you make about yourself. Instead, challenge them and examine them carefully for faulty thinking. Look as objectively at the matter as you possibly can. If you still end up in the pits, call on a trusted friend to help you sort things through and test your thinking.

(9) Believe that people like people who like themselves. No doubt people don't like people who have big heads; but it is *not* true that people don't like people who like themselves. Quite the contrary. People are not attracted to people who put themselves down. But people *are* attracted to people who feel good about themselves and respect themselves as persons of worth and value.

"Birds of a feather flock together." An old saying, but true nevertheless. Seek out people who project a positive self-image, people whose demeanor and manner tell you that they love themselves. You may be able to learn much about a positive self-image through those associations.

(10) Accept positive feedback graciously. It may be socially acceptable to play the game of "false humility," but people may also be put off by having their compliment to you severely discounted or even rejected. If I say to you, "You played that piece very well," and you reply, saying, "Oh, it was nothing," I may be offended for two possible reasons: (1) I may hear you say, "Bill, you are wrong. You may think I played well, but you are mistaken. I reject your evaluation." (2) I may hear you say, "My good man, what you just heard is a mere 'drop in the bucket' compared to the way I *can* play."

Graciously accept positive feedback—with a simple, sincere "Thank you," or with an embellishment added: "I'm glad you liked my playing." Store the compliment away in your treasure box of memories.

(11) Cherish your body. Physical health is important to feeling good. If you are developing your love for yourself you will love your body; you will cherish, respect, and care for it.

Seven basic rules of good health emerged from studies made by researchers at the University of California—Los Angeles School of Public Health. Other investigators following the nearly 7000 adults in UCLA's study confirmed the value of abiding by these basic rules. Here they are:

Seven Basic Rules of Good Health[1]

• Do not smoke. Simply read the warning on a package of cigarettes or in printed advertising for cigarettes: "The surgeon general has determined that cigarette smoking is dangerous to your health."

• Drink alcohol only in moderation. Overindulgence and abuse of alcohol is severely detrimental to body organs and functions.

• Maintain appropriate weight. There are many interpretations as to what is "proper" weight. Consult your physician to determine what is the ideal weight for you.

• Eat breakfast. The word itself indicates its importance: you have been fasting for the past 10 hours or so, and now you need to break that fast with a meal that will provide fuel to get your "vital juices" flowing for the day.

• Don't eat between meals. "In-between snacks" simply add unnecessary calories and upset bodily functions related to digestion and metabolism.

• Exercise regularly. Physical exercise is necessary to good health. Brisk walking remains the cheapest, most simple, and most effective form of exercise.

• Get 7 or 8 hours of sleep daily. Sleep is necessary to rebuild our bodies and it refreshes us.

(12) Talk to yourself. Remind yourself verbally that you're OK. You count. You're a person of worth and value. Give yourself positive messages. Compliment yourself for your successes and celebrate your gains in your journey. When you backslide into an old, self-disliking thought or behavior, first of all accept it, but then talk to yourself about how it happened and how you might prevent it from happening again. Forgive yourself and move on in your journey to a deeper love of yourself and a healthier self-image.

It will help to say to yourself: "Accentuate the positive," "You're a worthwhile person," "You have many talents." Write these phrases and others like them on small cards and place them in a variety of places at home or in your car so you will come across them several times a day. These reinforcers will help you keep on a positive track about yourself and help prevent you from getting bogged down in negatives.

Finally, in all this it is important to remember that you are cultivating one of the most significant factors in the joy of feeling good.

Key Number 2

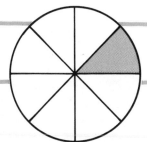

Evaluate Your Values

Finding your path between "anything goes" and "everything is black or white."

*W**e hold these truths to be self-evident, that all men are created equal, that they are endowed by their Creator with certain unalienable rights, that among these are life, liberty and the pursuit of happiness."*

This quotation from the American Declaration of Independence speaks of values. It declares that our nation's values include the right to live freely and to pursue happiness. Values are what we stand for, what we believe in, and things for which a great many Americans have given their lives.

Values are necessary—not only for nations, but for all of us as individuals. In the process of growing up we each develop a value system—a collection of values that speaks to virtually every aspect of our lives. It is a collection of beliefs, principles, standards, qualities of intrinsic importance, and matters of meaning and significance. Our values form the code and canon by which we live our lives.

What Is in a Value System?

Values have to do with our position on everything from the very profound things of life to the very mundane. To get an idea of the dimensions and content of your value system, try to answer the following questions.

Ten Questions for Determining Your Value System

(1) What do you stand for?
(2) What do you believe in?
(3) Is there anything for which you would lay down your life?
(4) What is important to you?
(5) What is unimportant to you?
(6) What do you believe is the point or purpose of life?
(7) What do you want to hold on to?
(8) What are you willing to give up?
(9) What do you choose to spend your time and energy on?
(10) What are your religious beliefs?

Trying to answer these questions for yourself is important and is an exercise that could easily occupy you for the next week. Our answers to these questions give us insight into the multitude of principles, regulations, formulas, beliefs, standards, rules, maxims, norms, and criteria by which we live our lives.

Look at the Continuum

The extremes along the value system continuum are striking. At the one end is virtual psychopathy and anarchy, where there are *no* values. You do anything you want, following the path of least resistance. Anything goes.

At the other end is absolutism. This is a value system in which every aspect is either black or white: fixed, unalterable, totalitarian, and established forever. It is monolithic and immovable. The values have always been and will be forever.

We may never have actually encountered these extremes in their purity, but chances are we have all been familiar with people whose values seemed to come very close to them. Some people talk and act as though they live by an absolute and fixed value system, while others live in such a wild, rebellious, or even sociopathic way that they seem to have no value system whatsoever.

Feeling good involves finding a midpoint between the two extremes. What we need is a value system that is based on a strongly established foundation but embellished with flexibility.

Be Sure Your Value System Is Yours

Some years ago I taught an ethics course for student nurses. One of my objectives was to help the students determine their own value systems. At the beginning of the course I said to them, "You all have a value system right now. But neither I nor you know how much of that is yours. So we're going to discuss, debate, dialog, role play, and probably quarrel over ethical matters, morals, and values this whole year. I am not so much concerned about what your value system looks like at the end of the year—in fact, it could look exactly the same as it does right now. But I'll tell you this—at the end of this course, whatever your value system is, it will be yours."

The Story of Bob

Bob grew up in a small town north of Boston. His home environment was a happy one—secure, uncomplicated, and sincere. He remembers that it was his mother who was most influential in shaping his life, teaching both by precept and example what she believed a godly, responsible, and loyal life should be. She demonstrated those dimensions well, he recalls, and it was from her example that he developed his deep sense of integrity.

From early on Bob liked numbers and the concepts around numbers. He seemed also to have inherited an interest in business from his father. So when he considered his future in discussions with his school counselors, Bob decided to pursue a career in business finance.

It proved to be a correct choice. Academically he did well, but more importantly, he was delighted with the work. He was a natural for it. He earned a bachelor's degree, a master's, and then launched into the world of work. His first job was with a restaurant chain. Then two years later he took a position with a large trucking company. This required a move out of his home area, but Bob was now on his way, moving up the corporate ladder.

Soon Bob had made five corporate jumps, each move meaning greater responsibility and greater financial reward. He had become employed as chief financial officer for a sizeable manufacturing firm.

But when I first met Bob he was deeply discouraged, despondent, and anxious about his marriage and his future. He had quit his job five months earlier, had had no income during that time, and hadn't been able to get another job. "I don't know what I'm going to do," he said. "I can't seem to get off dead center."

As we talked together and Bob unfolded his story, I began to get a sense of the man's deep integrity. He had quit his last job because the president of the firm had suggested that he do certain accounting manipulations which would allow the company to appear more financially successful than it was. While there was nothing illegal about what the president suggested, Bob saw it as immoral—it would have been unfair, would have given an inaccurate picture of the company, and could potentially have misled many people.

When Bob told his boss that he would not do what he wanted done, the president said to him, "Either you do it, or you're out." And so it was that Bob quit his job.

Five months later, Bob talked about how his thoughts had been going to his other jobs, his first job, his home, and his mother, who had impressed him so strongly with what she believed was important in life. "Something she said to me many times has been troubling me. When I was a boy, she would talk with me about my future, and work, and success, and achievement. She would say to me, 'Bob, the true sign of loyalty and success is to go to work for a good company, work diligently for them all your years, and then retire after 50 years and receive a gold watch.' "

Well, Bob hadn't done that. And now it was eating away at him so badly that his resources were sapped and his energy to present himself as a desirable and capable professional to a potential employer was just about dried up. His self-image was severely battered, his spouse was finding it hard to love him because he had fallen out of love with himself, and he felt as if he was walking down a dead-end street.

The values Bob adopted from his mother were both helpful and destructive. The value of honesty and integrity supported Bob in his decision to refuse to do what he considered immoral. This value was a high priority for him—so high that he was willing to sacrifice his job to hold fast to it. "You simply cannot do a thing like he (the president) wanted me to do and live with yourself."

However, Bob's value that defined professional success for him turned out to be a hindrance. His need to work for the same company for 50 years virtually paralyzed him when he lost his job.

A Happy Ending

When Bob freed himself from having to live by values that were not truly his own, he could experience absolution for the guilt of betraying them. His positive self-image returned as he became free of his guilty feelings and as he discarded the belief that he was doomed to be an everlasting failure.

Bob never did go to work for another employer. Instead he established his own consulting firm (something he had wanted to do for a long time). He has since published articles in professional magazines and has coauthored a book. Who knows, maybe he'll even give himself a gold watch when he retires and be a "success" after all!

How Do Values Come About?

Most of us have our values established for us. In the process of growing up we are inundated with values from a wide variety of sources. We learn them from parents, teachers, relatives, playmates, our family (its heritage), our nationality, our socio-economic class, our faith system, television, movies, novels, our family's political views, and the trial and error experiences of life.

Sometimes the values from various sources conflict with each other and it is necessary to try to resolve the conflict. Without help, however, it is often difficult for a young person to do this. Most of the time we simply adopt the value offered by the source that we respect more or like more or want to please more.

There are some sound, basic values that we adopt, such as those in Christian faith and life. But there are a myriad of others we adopt regardless of their logic or whether or not they are outmoded, prejudiced, or make any sense.

Bob was 52 years old before he critically examined a value that nearly ruined him. Many of us fall victim to the same mistake.

Six Steps to Evaluate Your Value System

(1) Write out the "Ten Questions for Determining Your Value System" (from the beginning of this chapter) on separate pieces of paper. Write each question at the top of a page and allow the full page for your response. (There are no "incorrect" answers.)

(2) Think of answering these questions in terms of relationships: your relationship with others (family, friends, peers, neighbors, strangers, enemies), with your self, and with God.

(3) Try to recall where these answers came from. Did your parents give them to you? Did you think them up yourself? Did they come from learning in the "school of hard knocks?" Did you get them from the Bible? your church? schoolmates? teachers? a book written by a philosopher? a political rally?

(4) Mark with a red pencil all the statements on all the pages that, as you think more seriously about them, don't "set" quite right with you. Consider these statements more carefully and determine whether they are truly a part of *your* values or whether they came into your system without your giving them much thought, and they have just hung around—possibly giving you conflict without your even knowing it.

(5) Mark with a green pencil all statements that seem incompatible with any other statements on any of the pages. These will indicate values that are in conflict with each other in your system. These are some of the rascals that cause us to be so indecisive at times.

(6) Mark with a blue pencil all statements that do not seem to match the way you are living now. You have no doubt changed over the past 20 years. Maybe

you have some values that are a score of years behind you. Or perhaps it occurs to you that the values are still valid, but you are living in disregard of them.

The Value of Completing the Task

Evaluating your values requires time and effort. But I assure you, the payoff in terms of heightened self-awareness and self-understanding is worth every minute of time and every ounce of effort. People who have completed this process of evaluating their values have reported mild amazement at what they discovered. For many of them, long-standing mysteries were finally solved.

This process should help you realize that your midpoint on the continuum is in this case not so much a mid*point* as a mid*spread*. Perhaps you will find that some of your foundational values are closer to the absolute extreme of the continuum and appear as fixed and unchangeable. This would be particularly true of faith values. And this is as it should be. In a time when the only thing that seems certain is uncertainty and the only thing that seems constant is change, spiritual values form an immutable foundation. Jesus Christ is the same yesterday, today, and forever (Heb. 13:8).

A Word about Changing Values

While some of your values are to the absolute side of the midpoint, you may also observe that much of your value system is flexible. This is good because our values *need* to change as we move on in years and as the circumstances of life change.

I sometimes wish I had completed writing out answers to the "Ten Questions" every 10 years of my life so that I could place them side by side and see how my values have changed over the decades. It would be fascinating to compare what is important to me today with what I said was important when I was 20.

Priorities shift as the years pass. It is therefore necessary to establish values that have flexibility. For instance, the "mellowing" aspect of the second half of life requires a gradual shift in values from the more hectic first half. Being in "sync" with your value system rather than in conflict with it is a significant part of feeling good.

Values, Stress, and Feeling Good

When a stressful situation occurs or a critical incident happens in our lives, we try first of all to assess it, size it up, and do a brief analysis of it. How we choose to perceive the situation or the incident will depend on our value system.

This is the reason why two people can experience the exact same event and one may feel considerable stress while the other may hardly be moved by it. The first person perceived the event as a substantial threat. That person determined it was threatening because his or her value system said it was. "There are some important values that are being questioned by this event," says the value system. "You had better prepare yourself, because this is a significantly stressful event."

On the other hand, the second person was hardly disturbed by the event. That person concluded that it was not threatening because his or her value system said not to be concerned. "There is nothing in this event to question or challenge any values," says the value system. "So don't get too upset by it. This event is not significant or important."

We know that excessive stress can generate or contribute to many forms of illness. We depend on our value system to tell us how to perceive a potential source of stress or a crisis and consequently how to deal with it. It is tough enough as it is to have to face potential crises and stress-causing events, but if we have a value system that falls down on the job of assessing and analyzing events, we are really in trouble.

When value systems are unable to help us perceive and interpret an event, this is generally due to one of two reasons (or to both):

(1) Many of the values of the system may not be what we actually believe and espouse.

(2) Where conflicting values have never been resolved, we do not know what our value is, so we do not know where we stand.

Such situations are potentially dangerous. We actually experience "stress on stress." We feel the stress of an event and we want to try to interpret the event in terms of our values. "How much of me is being threatened? Is this a hurricane or just a strong wind?" But there is no clear answer. We don't know if we should be upset or not, or how upset.

Here is where a clear understanding and knowledge of your value system helps significantly. And it is helpful to learn how to prioritize, trade-off, and delay gratification.

(1) Prioritizing. When you face the dilemma of two valid values being in opposition, but both presenting reasonable cases for their being honored immediately, consider the ramifications and consequences, immediate and long-term, of each. Then determine, *in the context of your overall value system,* which should supercede the other, and rank them in that order.

(2) Trade-off. If you decide that boating down the eastern seaboard from New York to the Florida Keys is something you have yearned to do for years, and you decide that you *will* do it two years from now, you also have to decide what you will have to give up or sacrifice in order to be able to do it, timewise and moneywise. What will be the trade-off? What will you have to trade in order to achieve that goal?

Virtually the same process occurs in dealing with conflicting values. We find it necessary to sacrifice honoring part of one value in order to fully honor another which is in conflict with it.

(3) Delayed gratification. It is possible to delay honoring one of the two conflicting values when such a problem occurs. Very often you can determine this clearly when you evaluate your values even further and consider the ramifications and consequences, immediate and long-term, of each.

Our society has promoted immediate satisfaction and "Why wait?" to such an extent that many people have almost forgotten that the option of delayed gratification still exists. It does, and it can be very helpful to us as we face resolving a conflict in our values.

Evaluate Your Values

An important dimension of feeling good is to know as clearly as you can *where you stand*. When you say to me, "How are you doing, Bill?" and I reply, "Very well, thank you," a part of that answer comes from the good feeling of security that my value system gives me. When you do the work of evaluating your values, you *know* what *you* stand for, what *you* hold fast to, what is truly valuable to *you* and what you can let go. A sense of knowing where you stand can eliminate great amounts of stress in your life. You're clear, not hesitant—not a reed shaking in the wind or a boat adrift at sea without a rudder. Tough decisions can be much easier to make when you're clear on your values. And by evaluating your values you can experience more of the joy of feeling good.

Key Number 3

Care about Others

Finding your path between self-sacrifice and self-centeredness.

*M*any have laid a severe indictment of selfishness against the current generation by calling it the "me" generation. Some critics have termed ours a "couldn't care less" society. If we're not completely "looking out for number one," then we are at least concerned about "What's in it for me?"

At the other end of the continuum are those who actually sacrifice themselves in caring about others. By this I do not mean giving their lives to protect their loved ones or their nation—to die so that others may live. Rather, this extreme involves *needless* sacrifice of self—overcaring—when such behavior is detrimental not only to the one performing it, but often to the one or ones for whom it is done. This type of unhealthy caring is where the caregiver acts more out of personal needs than out of unselfish devotion to the welfare of others.

There is generally little question about the negative, even destructive effects of me-ism. Persons have been known to go as far as to sacrifice their family relationships and even betray friends and colleagues to accomplish their selfish ends. Once it was necessary for me to physically step between two brothers who were about to begin a fistfight in the Intensive Care Unit of our hospital, as they violently quarreled at the bedside of their dying father, arguing about who would take what out of the estate. Rather than show loving compassion to a man close to death, they spat rageful threats at each other designed to defend their self-interest.

There is little difficulty in spotting the damaging consequences of not caring at all, or caring too little about others. But fortunately there is a growing awareness of the potentially harmful effects of caring "too much." Words such as *codependent, enabling,* and *burnout* have become familiar. A codependent is a person who has developed an unhealthy pattern of relating to another or others, usually as a result of having been closely associated and involved with someone who was dependent. The close association and involvement often causes the codependent to develop an overbearing personality, a poor self-image, low self-esteem, a strong need to be needed, and a deep wish to control and reshape others. In their need to be needed, codependents put themselves in positions of suffering for the sake of others and find self-sacrifice to be their calling in life.

The word *enabling* refers to the behavior of someone who avoids intervening in the dependency (addiction) of a person with whom they are closely associated. They fail to confront the dependent person with the facts and consequences of his or her dependency. The terms *dependency* and *addiction* refer not only to alcohol and drugs, but to virtually anything that will allow a temporary avoidance of the pain of reality and an escape into a better, more comfortable experience. Compulsive gambling is an addictive behavior; there is also compulsive sexual activity, compulsive eating, compulsive dieting, working, cleaning, spending, etc. The "enabler," wishing not to offend, upset, or criticize the dependent person, looks after and covers for him or her. In overcaring, the enabler actually supports the other person's dependency.

Burnout has been called the "disease of the over-committed" and "the helper's occupational hazard." Burnout is a gradual physical, emotional, spiritual, and social breakdown as a result of a person's overextension in caring for others, along with a failure to take care of oneself. Overdoing caring generates stress in a person's life, and chronic stress is identified as the primary source of burnout.

Six Rules for Caring about Others (in Ways That Will Contribute to Feeling Good)

The following six rules can help you discover the important balance between the extremes on this continuum and find your appropriate midpoint between them.

Rule 1: Distinguish between caring that is appropriate and caring that is overcaring.

The natural extension of loving your self (Key Number 1) is caring about others. It is the nature of our human species to interact with others. We are not by nature loners. We seek to help one another, support one another, and care about one another.

Learn to become accepting of others. If you are accepting of yourself as you are, in your strengths and weaknesses, you will be able to accept others as they are. To accept people in the name of love and caring is to take them as they are without immediately laying plans and developing strategies to remake them into what you believe they ought to be. Accepting does not mean agreeing with, condoning, or reinforcing anything in others that is contrary to your values and integrity.

Sometimes people back off from the concept of accepting others as they are, believing that to do this would require that they abandon their values and integrity and become all things to all people, ending up being nothing to anyone. Quite the contrary. Loving others, caring about them, and accepting them helps give clarity and security to your own value system and encourages you all the more to cherish your heritage, your tradition, and what you stand for.

Continue to love and care for others through disagreement and conflict. Love and caring needs to be seen in disagreement and conflict. Simply because you love someone does not mean that you must agree with him or her in everything. And vice versa. Our uniqueness as individuals allows us to see things differently. As a result there will always be disagreements and conflicts. They are natural and unavoidable. Loving and caring for others can make conflict a creative and constructive experience instead of a harmful or destructive one.

Choose to spend yourself on others as well as your-

self. In the list of "Ten Questions for Determining Your Value System" at the beginning of Chapter 2, the ninth question asked, "What do you choose to spend your time and energy on?" If you answered those questions for yourself as I suggested, I hope you included "others" in your answer to question 9. This is not only because of our natural inclination toward gregariousness, but also for the sake of feeling good about life. It is in giving that we receive, and often we receive much more than we give. It is in spending time and energy on others that we receive joy from God. "I tell you the truth, whatever you did for one of the least of these brothers of mine, you did for me" (Matt. 25:40). Joy comes from sharing with others the love and caring we receive from God and feel for ourselves. Caring means that we consciously focus ourselves on causes that are outside and beyond ourselves, not *only* on our own interests.

Identify caring that has gone awry. It is possible to have too much of a good thing. Caring can get out of hand. When caring goes too far it becomes overcaring, and it is often done for the wrong reason.

Jan and Elaine were students in a training program that focused on clear communication, interpersonal relationships, and the development of counseling skills. Jan had suffered a severe disease in her youth and was physically handicapped as a result. She had learned over the years to take care of herself quite adequately. While she experienced some physical limitations, these did not hinder her participation in the course.

Elaine however, in her caring about Jan, took it upon herself to become Jan's caretaker and guardian. Elaine had grown up in an environment of strong religious education and was highly motivated to serve and take care of others. To Elaine, Jan appeared to be a prime candidate to receive extraordinary care, so she opened doors for Jan, offered to carry things for her, helped her with her tray in the cafeteria, and helped her on and off with her coat. Most of this helpfulness and caring was considered unnecessary by the others in the program. In most of these instances Jan appeared to be quite able to take care of herself.

After a few weeks of the caretaking, Jan confronted Elaine and asked her to stop. "I don't want to hurt you, and I believe you mean well," she said, "but your constant caring is overbearing. I don't need it, and furthermore it makes me feel like an invalid. Yes, there are times when I need some assistance. But I am not afraid or ashamed to ask for it; and I will."

Elaine's servant role and her need to help had gotten out of hand and was actually offensive. Her overcaring was not meeting Jan's needs, it was meeting Elaine's need to be helpful.

In this case the most helpful thing would have been if Elaine had first consulted with Jan before giving such care. Elaine made an assumption that was probably based on her religious education, but her assumption was erroneous.

Look for faulty thinking in excessive caring. Sandy is an attractive young woman of 35 who has been married twice, has a responsible position in a financial firm, and is currently struggling to shake loose from an intimate relationship with a man who disrespects and abuses her. I call her behavior a struggle because even though she intellectually realizes the lopsidedness of this relationship, she feels powerfully drawn to the man. He takes advantage of her, makes demands of her, and disrespects and abuses her, but she nevertheless believes she loves him and needs his presence. "I want to throw him out," she says, "but I don't want him to go away."

This scenario is virtually a carbon copy of her experiences with her two ex-husbands.

Why does Sandy continue in this self-defeating behavior, which to the objective observer appears to make no sense at all? It is because Sandy has become locked into a behavioral pattern of self-sacrifice and suffering that presently is the only way she knows how to relate. She began her "career" of such behavior by growing up in the home of an abusive father and a passive mother. She became the caretaker in this turbulent situation, looking after mother, brother, and sister. As is so often the case, when the adults did not act as adults, the child became the adult. Memories of her father's tyranny, unfaithfulness, and unreliability are vivid. The suffering, self-sacrificing role which she adopted in that household was the role that she sought when she left it for a new relationship. And it is the same role that she has continued to play throughout her life.

When children who grow up in dysfunctional households vow, "I'll never marry anyone like my mother (or father)," they usually do.

If you developed and matured in a household where you knew your parents loved you because they told you so, displayed appropriate affection, and gave you messages that told you they accepted you as your own person with your strengths and weaknesses, as an adult you will feel "at home" with people similar to them—people who generate within you feelings of self-affirmation, warmth, and security. You will tend to feel uncomfortable with and avoid people who overtly or covertly put you down, manipulate you, and attempt to take advantage of you.

However, if your home life while growing up was like Sandy's, where there was hostility, cruelty, over-dependency, manipulation, and disrespect, you will tend to feel "at home" with persons who even subtly suggest a representation of these attitudes and behaviors. You will feel more comfortable with such familiar relationships and will feel somewhat ill at ease with gentler, healthier, and more affirming persons. This is called the process of "unconscious selection."

Sandy's self-image has taken a thorough whipping over the years. This is the main reason why she remains in the role she is playing, even though intellectually she knows better. When she closes her eyes she is unable to picture any part of her own face. When someone calls her name at work, she reacts as if they were calling someone else. She can hardly believe that colleagues on the job consult her for direction and advice.

At the root of Sandy's difficulty is her innate need to be loved and cared about and to see herself as a person of worth and value. She did not receive appropriate forms of love and care, and her needs for nurture were not met. Her conclusion was that it was her fault for not trying hard enough. She thought that if she only did everything that was demanded of her or even more, she would be loved. So she became a nurturer, a caregiver par excellence. She thought, *If I love him enough and care about him excessively, he will become the man I want him to be*. The failure of this faulty thinking took Sandy's self-image into the depths.

Her growth in self-understanding over the hours we have been together encourages me to feel optimistic that Sandy will achieve a healthy love for herself and become freed from her self-sacrificing role. She has come to an intellectual understanding of many of the dynamics present in her situation and is slowly making progress. She continues to struggle, but she is on the way.

Rule 2: Realize that love for others can be tough as well as tender.

Sandy's overcaring to the point of self-sacrifice is a dramatic illustration of loving and caring too much. Her love was unhealthy for herself but it also allowed and even encouraged the men in her life to remain in their unhealthy states. It is the rule rather than the exception that in situations of dependency, exaggerated caring and love is more destructive than it is constructive. When this happens you know that something is wrong. Tender love needs to become tough love, and caring needs to be expressed through confrontation. To the extent that I do not work to help a dependent come to grips *with* his or her dependency, I enable (or subtly facilitate) the dependent *in* that dependency.

Review the 20 indicators of codependency:[2]

(1) My good feelings about who I am stem from being liked by you.
(2) My good feelings about who I am stem from receiving approval from you.
(3) Your struggles affect my serenity. My mental attention focuses on solving your problems or relieving your pain.
(4) My mental attention is focused on pleasing you.
(5) My mental attention is focused on protecting you.
(6) My mental attention is focused on manipulating you to "do it my way."

(7) My self-esteem is bolstered by solving your problems.

(8) My self-esteem is bolstered by relieving your pain.

(9) My own hobbies and interests are put aside. My time is spent sharing your interests and hobbies.

(10) Your clothing and personal appearance is dictated by my desires because I believe you are a reflection of me.

(11) Your behavior is dictated by my desires because I believe you are a reflection of me.

(12) I am not aware of how I feel, I am aware of how you feel. I am not aware of what I want, I ask what you want. If I am not aware, I assume.

(13) The dreams I have for my future are linked to you.

(14) My fear of rejection determines what I say or do.

(15) My fear of your anger determines what I say or do.

(16) I use giving as a way of feeling safe in our relationship.

(17) My social circle diminishes as I involve myself with you.

(18) I put my values aside in order to connect with you.

(19) I value your opinion and way of doing things more than my own.

(20) The quality of my life is in relation to the quality of yours.

These indicators point to overcaring—the overloving that is destructively self-sacrificing. Such caregiving harms the codependent as well as the dependent.

Understand the purpose of tough love. Tough love is "blowing the whistle" on the destructive dynamics of a relationship.

It may be difficult to imagine how love can be tough. But it is a tragic mistake to think that love can only be tender, accepting, and accommodating. True love refuses to encourage anyone in a destructive dependency.

Let love challenge the dependent. Enabling, fostering, nurturing, or facilitating an unhealthy dependency is not love. Love challenges the great seduction of the manipulative person. Love respects the self and the other so much that it will not allow the self to participate in being "used," nor will it allow the other to "use" it. In other words, I love and respect me and you so much that I will not allow myself to slip into the sin of codependency, nor will I allow you to sin against me. I have no power to change your behavior, but I will not allow it to continue to be perpetrated on me. Love does not speak out of hostility or aggression—love speaks out of assertiveness.

Decide if the excessive loving and caring is authentic or a cover-up. There is an insidiousness about codependency; it is so easy to justify behavior and say things like, "I don't want to hurt her feelings"; "I don't want to upset him or make him mad. He has enough to contend with at the office"; "I don't want to embarrass him"; "I need to protect her—she is so fragile." The powerful forces of denial can convince a codependent that statements such as these are expressions of "love that goes the extra mile" and "caring beyond the call of duty."

Determine if your caring is helping the cared-for one to more complete wellness. Is the recipient of the love and caring becoming a more whole person? Is he or she modifying hurtful behavior as a result of your love and caring? Is there "change for the better"? Is the cared-for one happier? more loving? more at peace?

Answer the question, Does my sacrifice of love give me a good feeling? Long before his wife's 50th birthday, Jim decided to do something extra, extra special to honor her and celebrate the occasion. After all, one is 50 only once. After pondering many possibilities, Jim decided to go all out. Instead of purchasing a new car, he would make his old one do for another year or so and he would use the money instead to buy his wife a beautiful gold bracelet. It was a sacrifice for Jim, but he felt on top of the world doing it.

The moment that his wife opened the package on her birthday was an experience that neither of them will ever forget!

Parents make great sacrifices for their children out of love. Spouses sacrifice for their mates out of love. Children sacrifice for elderly parents out of love. Authentic self-sacrifice carries with it a deep sense of fulfillment and satisfaction, not resentment or despair. If your answer to the question, Does my sacrifice of love give me a good feeling? is *no,* you need to reexamine what you are doing.

Rule 3: Surrender your need to control others.

Here we must seek a healthy midpoint between the extremes of overresponsibility and irresponsibility.

Avoid confusing caring with controlling. At the birth of a child, parents must assume 100% responsibility for the child, or else the child will not survive. As the years pass, parents must train their children to gradually take on more and more responsibility for themselves so that ultimately the children become fully responsible for their own lives. Parents cannot expect a three-year-old girl to find her way unaccompanied to a restroom in a crowded department store and then meet them at a designated place in the store in 10 minutes. On the other hand, parents can rightly expect a 15-year-old to do this without guidance and recommendations from them.

When we refuse to allow our children to assume progressively more and more responsibility for themselves as they mature, we confuse caring with control and love with manipulation. There is a high risk involved in letting go of a child (or anyone about whom you care), because it means you allow that person to have real responsibility. The temptation is to think that you "know better," that you don't want to see the person "get hurt or hurt others," or that you want to look out for the person because you care about him or her. But how much of other people's responsibility can you take on yourself? Any time you say, "I will control your life for you," you open the gates for an on-rush of stress.

Take the risk of letting go. "If I don't call the people on the committee two days before the meeting to remind them to attend, half of them won't show up." Helen was complaining about the behavior of a church committee she chairs.

"Furthermore, if I don't come early to get the coffee going, we won't have any coffee." She paused, then added quickly, "And if I don't take notes, there will be no minutes of the meeting."

I wondered aloud why she needed a committee if *she* did everything. She smiled but failed to find humor in the remark. I didn't blame her, because no one likes a smart alec. But my sarcasm did serve to bring into focus her "enabling." She chaired a committee of people who appeared to be irresponsible. But were they? It appeared that she had assumed a lot of responsibility for them because she cared about the successful functioning of the committee. But her overcaring and overresponsibility had turned into resentment.

"How many people are on your committee?" I asked.

"Six."

"Suppose at your next meeting," I suggested, "you nicely announce that you are going to abandon the practice of telephone reminders prior to each meeting and you are going to respect their ability to remember to get there. *And,* suppose you ask for a committee member to volunteer to prepare coffee for the committee, if in fact that is what the committee wants. *And,* suppose as chairperson you appoint a committee member to assume the role of secretary and take minutes of the proceedings of each meeting. If you did this, Helen, what do you suppose would happen?"

"I don't know," she said.

"Neither do I," I replied. "But it's worth taking the risk of letting go of control to find out. You can feel a lot less stress if you don't have to carry the responsibility for seven people. You can feel a lot better just carrying responsibility for yourself."

Examine "overlove" in intimate relationships. Sometimes a spouse will say, "If I love him (or her) enough (or more), he (or she) will change." Translated, this means, "If I love (care about) you enough, perhaps I can get you to do what I want." This assumes that you have the power and control sufficient to alter the life of another human being by yourself. Nothing is impossible, but this assumption is highly improbable.

Sometimes people believe that marriage has magical powers. "After we're married, he'll be different. I'll love him so much that he won't drink, take drugs, be lazy, expect to be waited on, or carouse any more." People who "love too much," believing they can control the life of another person, abandon the joy of feeling good just as much as those at the other extreme of the continuum who have no concern for others whatsoever.

Know what you can change and what you can't. I have observed many people who brought great loads of stress on themselves trying desperately to "get" mommy or daddy to show them that they loved and accepted them. Just a simple arm around the shoulder and the words, "You're OK, kid, and I love you," would have been enough. But it never happened.

To accept the reality of that is to accept the unacceptable. It demands letting go of the need to control. It requires a strong self-image, self-affirmation, and self-confidence. To live with less than perfection may be less than desirable, but it is a whole lot more comfortable than the heavy stress of trying to change the unchangable.

Rule 4: Forsake the temptation of messiahship.

A *messiah* is a savior. In Christian faith, the Messiah is Jesus Christ. In his crucifixion, Jesus suffered and died for human beings and took all their sin on himself. He rose from the dead, thus ensuring salvation—that human beings could be reconciled to God and justified before God (Rom. 3:21-26).

In everyday parlance, a messiah is a person who sacrifices himself or herself for the good of others. It is generally a negative or derogatory term implying that such persons consider themselves capable of figuratively replicating *the* Messiah.

These are the people who overlove and overcare, extending themselves sometimes to the point of exhaustion or breakdown. The syndrome of symptoms which self-sacrificing careers often manifest has come to be called burnout.

Understand burnout. The condition of burnout is usually associated with chronic stress. In burnout, you lose zest. You continue to function, but you simply go through the motions, and your capability for productivity is greatly reduced. Physically, your blood pressure may elevate and you may experience trembling hands and impotence. You may drink excessively and have irregular sleep patterns. Emotional symptoms of burnout may include exhaustion, boredom, apathy, depression, frustration, loss of self-control, and difficulty in making decisions. Self-esteem and self-confidence may deteriorate. Spiritually, you may begin to question your faith, your commitment, and your values. Prayer may become difficult and you may experience a sense of hopelessness.

Burnout may very well be the result of overloving and overcaring. An overcommitted person may succumb to the temptation to take on more and more responsibility for other people, more and more responsibility for work that "needs to be done." The temptation is to one's ego: "I can do it better than anyone else"; "If I don't do it, it won't get done"; "I will do it so I know it is done right." Basically a messiah declares, "I will sacrifice myself to save humankind."

WARNING: Overcaring can be harmful to your health.

Guard against martyrdom. Caring for others is important, and people need to feel good about doing good things for others. But if caring generates feelings of resentment, exhaustion, and abuse, then something is obviously wrong. Because we are self-centered, sinful human beings, we can even abuse love and caring. "Come, let us take advantage of the 'overlovers' and those who have such a need to care; let us walk all over them." And the overcommitted smile up through the heels of those who are walking all over them and say, "We're serving, we're loving, we're caring." They may be "happy servants" on the outside, but they are "suffering martyrs" on the inside.

"Now is my way clear, now is the meaning plain; Temptation shall not come in this kind again. The last temptation is the greatest treason: To do the right deed for the wrong reason."

—T. S. Eliot[3]

Overcaring people, such as I have described above, do what they perceive to be the right thing, but they do it for a wrong reason. While they appear at the extreme of self-sacrifice on the continuum, they are actually located at the other extreme of self-centeredness. Their good deeds, love, and caring arise out of motivations that are largely unconscious: self-fulfillment, manipulation, control, egotism, and the need to change others. These people need to become acquainted with their "darker selves" and discover ways to use their "shadows" more constructively. Key Number 4 will deal specifically with this issue.

The temptation to messiahship can be enticing. It will not however, enhance the joy of feeling good. Therefore the next rule is crucial in employing this third key:

Rule 5: Accept the fact that you can care for others only when you care for yourself.

This rule focuses on the strong need for balance between the extremes of this continuum. Temptations at both extremes are great and discipline is required to locate and maintain your midpoint. This is neither a recommendation to become self-serving and abandon your responsibility to love others as your self, nor is it a suggestion to adopt the philosophy of "looking out for number one." But it is a plea that you not get bogged down in overcommitment. In their book *The Caring Question* (Augsburg, 1983), Donald and Nancy Tubesing have treated this issue thoroughly and helpfully. Their book can help you strike a healthy balance between caring for yourself and others by learning to set priorities and organize your time and by developing a support group.

Examine and evaluate your motives. Examine yourself to see what might be there that wants to keep you closer to the extreme of self-centeredness and hold you back from loving and caring about others. Look for things that might be driving you close to or even beyond your limits of self-sacrifice. Make a list of your discoveries and work out a plan (perhaps with a trusted friend or a professional) that will help you bring the desirable aspects of the two extremes together to a midpoint and will maintain a balance between the two.

Take care of yourself. Guard against the self-deception that you can give and give without being refilled. Don't consider yourself some sort of demigod and deny your humanity, thus making yourself a prime candidate for burnout.

People in the helping professions have a particular problem with this issue. We consider ourselves dedicated and committed to caring for others, but the needs to be met seem endless and we easily push ourselves to provide more and more care. Because so many of us fear doing anything that might be considered selfish, we fail to be good to ourselves and take care of ourselves. Very often what we label as fear of being selfish is our fear of disapproval or our fear of being criticized or condemned for normal, legitimate forms of self-assertion.

- Provide yourself with time to meditate and pray.
- Provide yourself with time for exercise.
- Provide yourself with time for family involvements, for social development, for cultivating friendships.
- Provide yourself with time for diversions: hobbies, entertainment, fun, reading for fun, nonproductive goofing off.
- Provide yourself with small rewards for taking care of yourself.

Rule 6: Learn the art of saying yes.

Rule Number 5 is what gives you the ability to provide love and to give care—to say yes to the people who need caring concern, especially in our depersonalized society. If you take care of yourself you can love fully, and your caring about others will generate *good* feelings.

Recognize the need for warmth. In a depersonalizing society such as ours, caring for others is essential. When you go through your mail, don't you first sort out and open envelopes that have your name typed or handwritten on them? Then you probably follow that with envelopes where your name is on a label, or printed in such a way that you know it came from a mass-mailing list. Then at the very end come the envelopes addressed to Resident, Occupant, or some other impersonal description.

In an increasingly technological society there is movement away from traditional personal interaction to a highly sophisticated system of communication. We find it not only in industry, business, and the professions, but also in our homes, marriages, and families. Instead of a warm hug and a kiss, or even a hearty handshake, we pick each other up on our radar and, like two ships passing in the night, sound our horns and flash our lights—but keep our distance.

The growing distance between persons will not be bridged by cybernetics. Silicone circuits are no substitute for human touch. No video screen can ever match the moist eyes of a compassionate human face.

Recognize the difficulty of being close. There is almost a kind of mathematical formula at work in giving love to others and caring about them. This formula states that "the ease by which a person can be loved is directly proportional to the square of the distance of the love-receiver from the love-giver." In other words, the farther away a person is, the *easier* it is to love that person.

For example, it is not too difficult to love a starving Asian child, a homeless person in a large American city, or a destitute individual in an Appalachian mountain town. We can accomplish that rather easily with prayers ("God help them"), thoughts of compassion ("Those poor people"), and monetary gifts ("Here's *my* contribution"). We can give that love and extend that caring without leaving the comfort of our living rooms.

On the other hand, how easy is it to love—right there in the same living room—a spouse who has fallen in love with a job and is having an affair with it; a husband or wife who feels increasingly unfulfilled and is becoming increasingly irritable; or a child who is becoming less and less accountable and more and more sarcastically independent; or a parent who dictates your life in an authoritarian fashion?

Or go outside your living room and try loving the neighbor behind you whose dog barks every morning between 2:00 and 3:00 A.M. Or try loving the competitor who is wiping you out with his advertising tactics. Or try loving the "perfect" wife and mother who regularly reminds you that there are no problems in *her* family.

Overcome the obstacles. There can be many obstacles to loving those close by, but you can deal with those obstacles in at least four ways:

(1) *See* the person to be loved as acceptable regardless of what he or she does or is. Based on your acceptance of yourself in your strengths and weaknesses and on your desire that others accept you as you are, accept this person close by and extend care to him or her.

(2) *Remember* the power of love and care. Caring for others and feeling cared for by them is one of the most important factors in the joy of feeling good.

(3) *Pray* for support from God and others in reaching out to extend love and care. Discipline is needed in reaching out, so be ready to accept all the help you can get.

(4) *Know* that in reaching out in love and caring you are less likely to dwell on your own problems. When we focus on caring for others, we decrease our preoccupation with our own burdens.

Invest your self. When you love yourself and see yourself as a person of value, you know the importance of investing yourself in other people. Love, however, is high-risk investment. There is no guaranteed return. The prospectus on a new common stock offering from a corporation usually paints a rather uninspiring picture of the company and its products. The prospectus is factual, without any window trimmings. This is by design, of course, so that potential investors are not seduced by glowing hints and questionable promises.

Love is a high-risk investment; you could lose your shirt—and more. You could love and not be loved in return. Love can only be unconditional. All you can say is, "I love you." You cannot say, "I love you if you do this, don't do that, are this, are not that, etc." When you love, you become vulnerable; you *make* yourself vulnerable. That is why the pain of love is the most intense pain one can know. You have made yourself vulnerable, open, and undefended. You have not kept up the normal defenses that protect you from being hurt by others and by the circumstances of life. Your very self is wide open.

Realizing the high risk of loving and caring, people may choose to remain on the self-centered side of the caring continuum. This is unfortunate, because even though the risk of loving is high, the potential for great reward is real. But if we are not willing to pay the price of investing ourselves in others, to willingly become vulnerable to the one loved and cared about, and choose instead to play it safe, we will never experience any of those goodies. When there is no risk there is no reward.

Investing myself in you means that I will give you my self as unselfishly as I can. I will give you my attention, interest, concern, and compassion—all the signals that tell you I care about you.

Give compassion and empathy in your caring. Empathy is the capacity and willingness to see the world through another person's eyes. It is to move into that person's skin and to the best of your ability allow yourself to experience the world as that person experiences it. It is the free giving of warmth and tenderness without any desire to possess. Compassion is the deepest and most authentic caring you can give.

When you care for someone you must be your real self, willing to invest yourself with all your strength and vulnerability, achievements and failures, and goodness and evil, with no need to pretend to be something that you aren't.

Tell them now. You might think that it would be easier to give positive strokes than to express negative feelings, but for many people it isn't. So they don't.

In my work I have been with many families in situations of death. I have been impressed by the number of people who express regrets about not having shared their positive feelings for someone before that loved one died. A new widower says, "If only I had told her how much I really loved her. Now it's too late."

I decided that I didn't want to have to say that myself, so many years ago I began to practice the principle of "Tell them now." I *like* to tell people positive things about themselves while they are still alive. Obviously I *can't* tell them after they're dead. This way I can avoid a lot of regrets.

Flattery does not count. Having a hidden agenda or an ulterior motive is unfair. The motive should be love. For example: "Lou, I listened to you at the meeting yesterday, and I just want to tell you that I really admire and respect your ability to think on your feet. I think you've got a real talent for the impromptu, for putting words together, for just saying things well; and . . . I just wanted you to know that."

Make caring your style. Some years ago Michael Maccoby, a psychologist versed in management history and theory, wrote a book entitled *The Gamesman: The New Corporate Leader.* In that book he described the leadership model that had appeared to work most effectively during the '60s and '70s: a "gamesman" or manipulative entrepreneur who thrived on risks, competition, and the exhilaration of victory.

In a later book, *The Leader: A New Face for American Management* (Ballantine, 1983), Maccoby observed that the leadership model had changed as a result of social and economic shifts. The leadership model of the '80s still resembles the gamesman in having a playful approach to his or her work. However, the playfulness is not directed toward gaining personal advantage, but toward consideration of the needs and feelings of the people he or she leads. The leader's makeup is now such that his or her satisfaction comes from "informed benevolence," willingness to share power and caring about people.

Care about Others

A great part of the joy of feeling good comes from caring appropriately about others. Good words, good deeds, and a caring attitude toward others will do wonders for them. But you will derive a full portion of the same feelings as they do.

Key Number 4

Accept Your Dark Side

Finding your path between your angel and your devil.

P*lease take a few minutes to answer the following questions:*

Quick Quiz No. 1

	YES	NO
1. Have you ever said something to another person and then wished you could have somehow gotten the words back?	——	——
2. Have you ever said something you didn't intend to say?	——	——
3. Have you ever done something you had no intention of doing?	——	——
4. Have you ever heard yourself say, "I don't know what came over me; I just wasn't myself"?	——	——

5. Has anyone ever said to you, "You sure weren't your usual self"?   ___ ___

6. Has your spouse or a close friend ever said to you, "What got into *you*?"   ___ ___

7. Have you ever been shocked or frightened by thoughts that passed through your mind? Have you ever wondered where they came from?   ___ ___

8. Have you ever found yourself identifying with the "bad guy" in a movie or play? rooting for the villain? hoping the crook gets away?   ___ ___

9. Have you ever been caught up in watching a sports event and heard yourself shouting vengeful, even bloodthirsty statements?   ___ ___

10. Have you ever wanted to "wipe out" a reckless driver, a manipulative coworker, or a nonstop talker?   ___ ___

11. Have you ever been introduced to someone and then later said to yourself, "I don't know why, but I just don't like that person"?   ___ ___

12. Have you ever realized that you have condemned another person for doing something which you also do but justify in yourself?   ___ ___

13. Have you ever caught yourself daydreaming about performing unrighteous acts?   ___ ___

14. Have you ever blamed someone else for what you knew was your fault?   ___ ___

15. Do you have any prejudices against anyone?   ___ ___

I hope you answered yes to many of the questions in the Quick Quiz. If you did, it's a good indication that you are normal. It also indicates that you are at least *acquainted* with your "shadow self," that dark, hidden counterpart to the image you daily present to society.

Your Shadow and Feeling Good

Human beings are a rather interesting blend of opposites. For example, they display greed and charity, loyalty and treason, aggression and submission. Plain and simply, their behavior is both good and not good. However, we want to be whole and complete people; integrated, not disintegrated; unified, not pulled apart.

We used to believe (and unfortunately, some people still do believe) that the way to personal improvement was through the continuous infusion of goodness, righteousness, morality, purity, and innocence. It was suggested that people get better and better by taking on more and more of these virtues. And that was that! Both society in general and religious groups in particular have traditionally encouraged this view. Parents drill into their small children that they must "behave nicely" and not as little animals.

There is no question but what this approach can help, but it is only half the process. Parents usually do not have to tell children to "Be bad," but they do have to teach them to "Be good." But what do we do with all that other stuff—the not-so-good stuff? Do we avoid and have nothing to do with it (as if that were even possible)? Do we pretend it isn't there, denying it completely?

We have learned that the technique of adding only positive influences to yourself and deleting the negative ones does not work well. In fact it can lead a "nice" person into serious trouble.

In reality, in order for us to better cope with ourselves and with life, we need not only to grow in goodness, righteousness, morality, and holiness, but also to become aware of and incorporate into our personality those traits and characteristics that are dark and shadowy, and by most standards, undesirable or even evil. Another way of describing this would be to say, "I am not a complete person until I incorporate into my conscious self that dark side of my person (my *shadow*) which is every bit as much a part of me as is that bright side which I present to society (my *persona*)."

The Development of Shadow and Persona

Since our shadow has a degree of scariness about it, it is good to know that we are incomplete beings without it. Without a shadow we would be only two-dimensional creatures, too good to be true. Every human being has a shadow and we all come by it quite naturally. We are by nature creatures capable of both great good and great evil. Remember how Mother Goose puts it:

> There was a little girl, and she had a little curl
>   Right in the middle of her forehead;
> When she was good, she was very, very good,
>   But when she was bad she was horrid.

No doubt you will recall that one of the very first things you learned in the process of growing up was how to get what you wanted. Through the process of trial and error you learned that certain acts and behaviors obtained positive rewards and others obtained negative ones. Consequently you put out front, for everyone to see, those qualities, characteristics, and behaviors that got you positive rewards because they were acceptable to and affirmed by society. The opposite characteristics, qualities, and behaviors that society rejected were gingerly kicked down the cellar stairs of your psyche. You slammed a heavy door shut on them so they would be safely locked away and be unable to make an appearance before the public and get you into trouble.

You learned early on that life is invariably a compromise; that often you cannot do or be what your raw self would prefer. And so, in order to make it, you have to be more or less what is expected and acceptable. You learned to put on a "mask"—a persona— what you know isn't your whole, true self, but what is required of you in this civilized culture. Furthermore, you learned that you have to have a whole trunkful of these masks that you slip on and off, much like the quick-change artist who could change personalities at the wink of an eye.

The Influence of Home Environment

The growing-up experience of a person has much to do with the development of one's personal shadow and persona. There is an inverse relationship between the size of the shadow and the home environment in which the person was reared: the more expansive the milieu, the smaller the shadow; the more restrictive the milieu, the greater the shadow.

The Expansive Atmosphere

People who grow up in an expansive atmosphere—one that is open, accepting, nonjudgmental, nonlegalistic, compassionate, relaxed, confident, and structured with reasonable limits—have comparably less to suppress and repress and consequently do not develop massive shadows. They learn the fundamental customs and values of their families and societies, but they are comparatively free to be themselves within reasonable limits of responsible behavior. They learn appropriate expression of feelings (Key Number 6) and consequently do not have to suppress and repress them. Because they learn to be comparatively self-confident and develop a positive self-image and healthy self-love (Key Number 1), they are not as dependent on society's approval and may thus be less inhibited—but still within the bounds of propriety. Much of what would otherwise be included in the shadow side of their psyches is integrated into their personalities.

The Restrictive Atmosphere

On the other hand, people who grow up in a restrictive atmosphere—one that is tight, narrow, rigid, legalistic, closed, demanding, judgmental, prejudiced, tense, and oppressive—have comparably more to suppress and repress because of the multitude of "musts" and "dare nots" they encounter. There are so many thoughts they are not allowed to have, so many words they are not allowed to speak, and so many behaviors they are not allowed to perform; and these must all be suppressed and repressed. The value of society's approval is significant in this type of milieu. There is little room for curiosity or experimentation; consequently these dynamics must be relegated to the shadow side. Spiritual experience in such a milieu is often a legalistic form of piety that demands suppression and repression of much of what is natural to the human experience.

The Shadow and Behavior

A person developing in such a restrictive atmosphere is highly prone to developing a very large and intense shadow and a thick, often moralistic persona. The theory of opposites is at work here: the more moral I appear in my persona, the greater is the potential for evil in my shadow. Also, I will be likely to deny the existence of my shadow because I have so successfully covered up my evil tendencies. Unfortunately, the person who most vehemently denies having a shadow counterpart is the one most vulnerable to its power and the one most likely to be overcome by it.

Most of the time, most of us do a rather decent job of keeping our shadow under control, keeping that antisocial "devil" locked away in the cellar of the psyche. But occasionally, for reasons we can't explain, it manages to slip under the door and sneak up the steps and embarrass us. Or else it suddenly crashes through the door and bolts into society's presence with some antisocial act that will get us into serious trouble. The shadow's emergence can be seen in a mere slip of the tongue (saying something you never intended to say) or in a tragic, antisocial act (assault, homicide).

REMEMBER:

The more I deny that there is a dark, unseen part of me, the more vulnerable I am to being overcome by it.

The more willing I am to admit and accept the potential for evil in me, the less likely I am to act out that evil.

Six Ways to Get Better Acquainted with Your Dark Side

(1) Solicit feedback from those who know you well. While we may be fairly blind to our own shadows, we can readily see the shadows of other people. Likewise, others can see ours. Those who know us most intimately are those who can see our shadow tendencies most clearly because they have seen us in a variety of settings under a variety of conditions.

If you are married, your spouse would be the most appropriate person to hold up aspects of your darkness for you to see. Quite possibly your spouse has already done this, but you have probably rejected it. Shadow material is more not-nice than nice, so we are much more apt to reject it than buy into it. If I solicit shadow feedback from my spouse and she says, "You don't realize it Bill, but you are rather short-tempered," I will probably not immediately jump at that and say, "Thank you. It's good to know that; now I can do something about it." Rather I will probably say, "There you go again. You always make something out of nothing."

If you are not married, a close friend or companion would be in a position to give you similar feedback. However, if you don't intend to do anything positive with the feedback you receive from people who know you well, don't solicit it. You will only entrench yourself more deeply in the belief that you really are what you appear to be, and that you really do not have a darker side (which spouse and friends can clearly see).

(2) Examine slips of the tongue and slips of behavior. Slips of the tongue occur when for some reason the governor that controls the shadow's mouth goes to sleep and the shadow speaks rather than the persona. You say something "wrong" or something you "didn't mean" or something you never intended to say publicly. The slip is usually more accurate (more truthful) than what your persona would have said. (We fool ourselves so easily.)

A friend shows you a painting that he or she has just purchased. You unconsciously assess it as being a piece of trash. You want to be polite and say, "Oh, that's just adorable." Instead, it comes out, "Oh, that's just abominable." You want to run from the room, rip out your tongue, and disappear; but what would be more helpful than any of the above would be to realize that your shadow has spoken and has, in a very embarrassing way, informed you that you need to pay more attention to it.

Slips of behavior are quite similar in their dynamics.

I may do something that is inappropriate and be highly embarrassed by it. I apologize and say, "That is absolutely the last thing I wanted to do." Most likely it was *exactly* what I wanted to do, have often wanted to do, but would never *dream* of doing. Again, for some reason the shadow governor was asleep at the switch, and at that precise moment I "acted out" my shadow.

Among other things, our shadow is everything we don't want others to know about us and everything we don't even want to know about ourselves. Our shadow is everything we don't want to be and do and everything we would dearly *love* to be and do, but don't dare. It is understandable then that after such "slips" we would say things like, "I don't know what got into me," "I don't know what came over me," or "I just wasn't myself."

It is also helpful to look at experiences where you were perceived differently than you intended to be. Once again your shadow was probably at work. For example, while greeting parishioners at the church door following the close of the worship service, a pastor was told by three persons, each independent of the other, "Nice sermon, pastor. You really gave it to them this morning." The pastor was dumbfounded. He preached on grace and forgiveness. Yes, there have been times when he would have *liked to* "give it to them," but. . . .

(3) Review what you "can't stand" in other people. Set aside a block of time, take a few sheets of paper, and write down a list of all the things you don't like in other people—traits, habits, characteristics, mannerisms, attitudes, beliefs, behaviors, etc. When you have completed the list, go back and review it, underlining with blue pencil all the items that you not only don't like but that you consider disgusting and despicable. Finally, review the collection of items underlined with blue pencil and then underline again with red pencil all the items that you find absolutely maddening and infuriating.

There you have it. Meet a fairly accurate representation of your personal shadow. We tend to see in others the nastiness that we refuse to see in ourselves, so the list should be helpful in coming face to face with a representation of your personal shadow.

By the way, always get a second opinion and even a third on insights from these exercises. Suppose your spouse gives you feedback to the effect that you sometimes appear arrogant in your relationships and encounters. Add to that your conscious awareness that this is the absolute last way you want to appear. Further, it turns out that arrogance is one of the traits in others that you find absolutely unbearable. Then it is very likely that arrogance is one of your shadow traits. But get a second and third opinion. Consult friends and colleagues who know you fairly well. Say, "Frank, I've been working on trying to get to know myself a little better and I seem to have discovered that I might have a tendency to appear arrogant at times. You know me. Please be honest with me. Have you ever perceived me that way?" If Frank *is* honest he will either corroborate your finding or reject it.

(4) Note with whom you identify in drama, novels, TV, and films. When we lived in Boston several years ago, there was once a small item in the newspaper about a man who had been arrested at a theater the

night before. I cannot recall the title of the play, but in the drama the characters of hero and villain were clearly identified. It appears that this man became so engrossed in identifying with the villain that when the hero was about to do the villain in, the man jumped from his seat, ran down the aisle, leaped on the stage, and physically attacked the hero. The article concluded, "He was detained by stagehands until the police arrived."

Remind yourself to become more aware of the identifications you make with various characters in drama. Note whom you are admiring, whom you are rooting for, how "viciously" you are rooting for him or her (for example, at a sports event), whom you don't like, and why. This will provide another glimpse of your shadow.

(5) Observe shadow activity in your dreams, daydreams, and fantasies. What do you think about when there is nothing to think about?

People often claim they do not daydream or fantasize, but I believe this is only their perception and really not the case. Where do your thoughts go when they are not directed by your consciousness? How many times have you caught yourself imagining "scenes" that shocked you? Have your mind's wanderings ever carried you into "dramas" that led you to say to yourself, "Thank heavens people can't read my mind!"?

Dreams may provide us with aspects of our shadow. Our shadow often appears in dreams as a dark and sinister figure, usually quite indistinguishable. There are no clear features, but the blackness and mere form are intimidating so that the dreamer instinctively feels fear. The shadow will often pursue the dreamer, and if the dreamer can turn in the dream and face the shadow the dreamer may become aware of his or her own shadow dimensions. Observe the actions, behavior, and words (if any) of the shadow figure.

(6) Examine the "Dr. Fell" syndrome.

I do not love thee, Doctor Fell.
The reason why I cannot tell;
But this alone I know full well,
I do not love thee, Doctor Fell.

—Thomas Brown

The rhyme speaks to the experience of not liking someone but not knowing why. You may be introduced to someone by a person who is a mutual acquaintance. Later, in privacy, your friend asks you how you liked this person. You reply, "OK, I guess, but there's something about him that I *don't* like, and I honestly can't put my finger on what it is."

What is probably happening is this: you are sensitive to an undesirable trait in this "new" person which, unknown to you, is also a part of your own personality. But because you are unconscious of it in yourself you cannot clearly identify it in him or her. All you "know" is that there is *something* about this person that is disturbing to you.

Next time this happens to you, share your confusion with the mutual friend who introduced the person to you. Quite possibly he or she knows you both fairly well. Ask your friend if there is any rather outstanding trait evident in the person which your friend also sees in you, but of which you may be unaware. Quite possibly you will get another glimpse of your shadow.

Four Options for Dealing with Your Shadow

Suppose you become familiar with your dark side and have good insight into your shadow self. What is the most helpful and constructive way to deal with it? There are four options, only *one* of which is desirable.

Option 1: Identify with your shadow and live it out. This would be to *become* criminality personified, which is one extreme on the continuum. This would be to find that potentially evil self which you have discovered so desirable that you *become* that self and act it out. This is essentially the choice that was finally made by Dr. Jekyll in Robert Louis Stevenson's story, *Dr. Jekyll and Mr. Hyde*. The worthy and benevolent doctor invented a potion that would enable him to turn into his opposite, Mr. Hyde. Dr. Jekyll believed this would allow him the "pleasures" which he could not enjoy in living out the persona of Dr. Jekyll. Dr. Jekyll's Mr. Hyde became more and more evil until the behavior culminated in murder. Jekyll had totally identified with his shadow counterpart and had in fact become that person. This option is totally unacceptable.

Option 2: Deny its existence. This second option is no better than the first. It could be compared to cutting your head off to get rid of a headache. It is a very dangerous option because, as I have noted, this makes you extremely vulnerable to being overcome by your shadow, sometimes in its raw, archetypal power. However, the option is very tempting because it seems so easy. If you deny that you have the potential for great evil within you, then you don't have to come to grips with that dimension of yourself. You believe that you are indeed what you appear to be, and nothing more. And that may be quite satisfactory to you.

There are entirely too many horror stories about the criminal behavior of people whose personas were virtually pure innocence and whose shadows overcame them in a mere second of time. There are common elements in the majority of these cases. The person is usually an outstanding individual, known by friends and neighbors for his or her uprightness and innocence, a shining example of goodness. Suddenly, and for no known reason, the person is overwhelmed by a power of evil, and the result is murder, often multiple murder. After the fact, the person is dazed, doesn't know what came over him or her, and friends and neighbors who knew the person say they "can't believe that he (or she) could possibly have done a thing like that."

Such comments indicate how very difficult it is to accept (and how ready we are to deny) the potential for great evil within us. Had the person who committed the crime been a hardened criminal, it would have been "understandable." But he or she was an upright, righteous person. "I can't believe it" means "I don't want to believe it. I want to deny" that he or she did a thing like that.

Option 3: Project it. The third option is no better than the first two. We know that one of the easiest ways to get rid of something we don't want is to throw it away. We don't want the contents of our shadows inside ourselves, so we throw them onto others: children, spouse, significant others, groups, inanimate objects, an enemy, foreigners, other races, nations, etc. If I project my greediness onto you, I will clearly see it in you (however slight), while I remain blind to it in me (however great).

Jesus often used exaggeration when he wanted to make a point. In teaching people to accept their own darkness and not project it onto others, he said,

"Why do you look at the speck of sawdust in your brother's eye and pay no attention to the plank in your own eye? How can you say to your brother, 'Brother, let me take the speck out of your eye,' when you yourself fail to see the plank in your own eye? You hypocrite, first take the plank out of your eye, and then you will see clearly to remove the speck from your brother's eye" (Luke 6:41-42).

Option 4: Embrace it and use it creatively. The only acceptable option is to accept your darkness as the part of you that it is. It involves saying to your shadow, "You are indeed as much a part of me as is the bright person I put before society. I respect your power and I acknowledge you as mine. You will, however, realize that as long as the power of light is greater than the power of darkness (John 1:5), you will be the driven and I will be the driver. With the help of almighty God I will control you and resist your temptation." By doing this you put a bit in your shadow's mouth, a bridle over its head, and use it creatively. You find your way to balance and integrate the opposites of persona and shadow, of "angel" and "devil."

How to Bring the Opposites Together

Jesus gave very sound advice to his disciples when he prepared them to go out two by two on their first mission of healing and teaching. He knew that they were bound to meet resistance to their message, particularly if they naively expected their audiences to be eager to hear their words and take up the new "way" that Jesus was declaring. So Jesus said to them, "I am sending you out like sheep among wolves. Therefore be as shrewd as snakes and as innocent as doves" (Matt. 10:16). He advised them to take both extremes and bring them together into a unified whole.

The extremes on our continuum are angel and devil. Those are symbolic characters, but fitting. To be angelic is not to be human. Those who deny their shadow present themselves in inauthentic goodness. They are too good to be true, and in fact they aren't true. Balance is found by bringing the two opposites together. To paraphrase Jesus, "Neither one nor the other alone is desirable; take both and be whole. Bring together the innocence of doves and the wisdom of serpents and you will be equipped for your task."

Take the opposites that you have discovered in your persona and shadow and write them out on a piece of paper side by side as on a continuum. For example:

PERSONA ———————————— SHADOW

Philanthropy ———————————— Greed

Generosity ———————————— Covetousness

Modesty ———————————— Arrogance

Compulsiveness ———————————— Laziness

Innocence ———————————— Lust

Prudishness ———————————— Libertinism

Peacefulness _____ Aggressiveness

Submissiveness _____ Rebelliousness

Fastidiousness _____ Sloppiness

Achievement _____ Wastefulness

Sweetness _____ Anger

Kindness _____ Callousness

Control _____ Irresponsibility

Find the potential good in what appears to be bad and the potential bad in what appears to be good. Temper each quality with its opposite; for example, see how modesty may be tempered by arrogance and arrogance by modesty so that a healthy balance of assertiveness may be the result. Likewise, see how compulsiveness may be tempered by laziness and laziness by compulsiveness so that a healthy midpoint of ambition may be the result. Always seek out the positives of the qualities and focus on them.

Five Reasons to Accept Your Dark Side

Much of our cultural background encourages us to deny the fact that we have a shadow at all. Here are five good reasons to accept the dark side of yourself:

(1) You will be a more authentic person. A greater awareness of your shadow and integration of it into your consciousness makes for a much "thinner" persona. You become less artificial and more genuine and transparent. You become comfortable with dimensions

of yourself which you perceived as objectionable before and about which you had to pretend. You become more "real"— someone you can accept and love (Key Number 1).

(2) You will be more "in charge" of your life. The better we know and understand ourselves, the better we can control our behavior and our lives. *We can do nothing about that of which we are unaware.* The more clearly we see the dimensions of our dark side, the better able we are to make conscious decisions to resist our shadow's temptations. We no longer have to be at the mercy of an unknown dictator.

(3) You will be better able to accept others. Accepting the fact of our own darkness clearly helps us accept the fact of our imperfection. This makes our acceptance of others much easier. We no longer have to expect others to be perfect because we know and accept our own imperfection. We are more tolerant of their weaknesses and shortcomings and we are more willing to accept them as they are.

(4) You will be freed from your need to project. A willingness to accept our own shadow means we no longer have to throw it onto others and cause them to bear our burdens. We accept responsibility that we used to project; we no longer blame others for our errors and shortcomings. We begin to see the world in a different way—no longer as a mirrored reflection of our own projections, but as it really is.

(5) You will experience grace in a new and greater sense. To realize the reality of our dark side and to become aware of the magnitude of our potential for

evil makes God's acceptance of us as we are more dear to us than ever before. To think that God still loves me, in spite of all this! The grace of God becomes more than a mere theological doctrine. God's grace *is* amazing!

Key Number 5

Realize Your Capability

Find your path between sloth and workaholism.

A good way to begin our discussion on realizing our capabilities is to look at Jesus' parable of the talents in the gospel of Matthew:

"Again, [the kingdom of heaven] will be like a man going on a journey, who called his servants and entrusted his property to them. To one he gave five talents of money, to another two talents, and to another one talent, each according to his ability. Then he went on his journey. The man who had received the five talents went at once and put his money to work and gained five more. So also, the one with the two talents gained two more. But the man who had received the one talent went off, dug a hole in the ground and hid his master's money.

"After a long time the master of those servants returned and settled accounts with them. The man who had received the five talents brought the other five. 'Master,' he said, 'you entrusted me with five talents. See, I have gained five more.'

"His master replied, 'Well done, good and faithful servant! You have been faithful with a few things; I will put you in charge of many things. Come and share your master's happiness!'

"The man with the two talents also came. 'Master,' he said, 'you entrusted me with two talents; see, I have gained two more.'

"His master replied, 'Well done, good and faithful servant! You have been faithful with a few things; I will put you in charge of many things. Come and share your master's happiness!'

"Then the man who had received the one talent came. 'Master,' he said, 'I knew that you are a hard man, harvesting where you have not sown and gathering where you have not scattered seed. So I was afraid and went out and hid your talent in the ground. See, here is what belongs to you.'

"His master replied, 'You wicked, lazy servant! So you knew that I harvest where I have not sown and gather where I have not scattered seed? Well then, you should have put my money on deposit with the bankers, so that when I returned I would have received it back with interest.

" 'Take the talent from him and give it to the one who has the ten talents. For everyone who has will be given more, and he will have an abundance. Whoever does not have, even what he has will be taken from him.' "

(Matthew 25:14-29)

While the point of this story has to do primarily with Christ's return, it also reinforces our intuitive awareness that we are meant to put to use the abilities we have or we will surely lose them. This is also one of the keys to the joy of feeling good—having the quiet satisfaction of making good use of our capabilities.

This key is used by people who are successful in employing their talents to the best of their ability. They feel reasonably fulfilled in what they are doing and being. They feel a sense of satisfaction and accomplishment that they have used their abilities productively. As with the first two servants in the story, they experience the voice of the master saying, "Well done, good and faithful servant."

Become an Imperfect Achiever

I like this phrase because it seems to encapsulate the balance point on this continuum. You realize your capability as you bring together the extremes of workaholism and sloth and strive to become an imperfect achiever. You try to use as much of your potential as possible, but that achievement is always imperfect—bounded by our human limitations.

In becoming an imperfect achiever you realize the capabilities within you and experience the full use of the talents, capacities, and potentialities that are common to all human beings and peculiarly unique to you. You do this without falling into the trap of workaholism, perfectionism, and compulsiveness. These extremes are detrimental to wellness because of the excessive stress they may generate in a person's life and the damage they may cause relationships. You also

avoid the slothful and disinterested end of the continuum. This extreme is detrimental because of the de-
pressive state it may generate and the irresponsible
behavior it may encourage.

**Feeling good involves finding the balance be-
tween settling for the path of least resistance
and pushing ourselves into an emotional and
physical breakdown.**

Ten Rules for Realizing Your Capability

Become an imperfect achiever! What will help you
do this? What will impede this? The following rules
are designed to help you find your own path between
the extremes on this continuum. I have found that the
best midpoint for one person may be far removed from
the best midpoint for another person. This is because
each of us is different and has different personal traits
and attitudes.

Rule 1. Establish your self-esteem.

This first rule takes us back to Key Number 1. You
need to believe in yourself and believe in your ability
to accomplish what you set out to do. You need to
have the confidence that you can indeed achieve your
potential. You need to exercise the power of positive
expectation.

I know of no philosophy that will help a person
achieve when that person is consistently doubting his
or her ability to do so. That sort of attitude will only

attract failure. No matter how hard you work for ac-complishment, if your thoughts are saturated with doubts about achievement and fears of failure, your attitude (disbelief in yourself) will kill your efforts, neutralize your endeavors, and make accomplishment impossible.

Remember from Key Number 1 that healthy self-esteem is built on our awareness of ourselves as val-uable and loved creations of God. It is God who has given us our individual abilities. As in the parable of the talents, God wants us to use these gifts to their fullest. God believes in us. Who are we not to believe in ourselves?

"Realizing your capability" is not some kind of superficial catch-phrase. It cannot be accomplished simply by repeating to yourself, "I can do it; I can do it." Instead, it is to take the Creator at his Word, to believe in God's promise to support us, and therefore *to believe in ourselves.*

Years ago when I was in seminary I experienced what seemed to me to be an overwhelming burden of work and study. Some days I seriously wondered if I could continue on in my pursuit of education and train-ing while working many hours a week. One night in the midst of this turmoil, I dreamed I was carrying a heavy sack over my right shoulder. I was not aware of going anywhere in particular; nor was I aware of what might be in the sack. I *was* aware, however, of the great weight of the sack and my doubts as to wheth-er I would be able to continue to carry it.

Then my father-in-law appeared in the distance, ap-proaching me. When I saw him coming close I was greatly relieved because I was sure he would help me by either sharing the burden, helping me carry it, or by taking the sack on his own shoulder for a while. However, as he got to my side he made no move whatsoever to help. Instead, he simply put his hand on my shoulder, looked at me, and said, "You can make it." That was the end of the dream.

To me the dream was both simple and very profound. It gave me great support and reinforcement. I saw that my father-in-law was a symbol of the wise, old man deep within myself reminding me that even though the going was rough and the load was heavy and I wondered if I could continue on, I could. Even though I was beginning to doubt whether I could achieve my goal and accomplish what I set out to do, I could.

I chose to believe that I could make it. And I did.

Rule 2: Identify your direction.

To get anywhere, you must strike out for somewhere, or you'll end up nowhere.

In order to realize your capability, it is necessary to specify what it is you wish to accomplish. Many people do not do this, and that turns out to be at least one reason why they feel dissatisfied, unhappy, and unfulfilled. It is true that you have to identify your direction and pinpoint your destination if you intend to realize your capability. Otherwise you end up in frustration and confusion.

Realizing your capability requires specific goal-setting. People are not self-fulfilled because they simply wandered into self-fulfillment. At some point they decided where they wanted to go and then decided how they would get there. The key to doing this is to *be specific.* It is one thing to wish that your life were more meaningful and quite another to first decide what "meaningful" means to you, then state specifically what would achieve that for you, and finally identify clearly your direction and map out paths to your goals.

This process is absolutely necessary in any effort to realize your capability. *If you don't know where you're going, any road will get you there.* And once you *get* there, you don't know where you are. I believe this is why so many people feel frustrated, confused, and unhappy. They may have a vague notion of where they would like to be going, but they have not clearly defined their destination(s). Having failed to do this, they are unable to select a road that will take them to where they want to go. So they keep moving and traveling, somewhat aimlessly, muttering, "There must be more to life than this."

The difference between wishful thinking and ambition is time and energy. Wishful thinking is a pleasant pastime for people who choose simply to let life happen. Ambition may be defined as the desire to use fully the abilities and talents you possess; the desire to achieve a particular end or goal.

Here is a bare-bones but sure-fire outline for identifying your direction as you seek to realize your capability.

Establish goals. Allow yourself plenty of quiet time to review where you are in your life and to determine and refine what you would like to accomplish. Make a list of your strengths and abilities. For instance: "I am especially sensitive to people's feelings." "I can think very systematically and logically." "I am secure and comfortable traveling to unfamiliar places." Make another list of your special personal skills: "I am gifted mechanically." "I am a skilled woodworker." "I grasp mathematical functions quickly." Make another list of skills and talents that you believe you have but which are underdeveloped or undeveloped and have never had a chance to be tested out. Finally, make another list of dreams, hopes, and "What I have always wanted to do" causes.

Once again, allow yourself *plenty of quiet time* to do this and to mull over these lists, add to them, and scratch things out. Allow yourself to delve deep, discover, remember, and evaluate. Out of this experience let a handful of goals crystalize—specific achievements you want to accomplish. Write them out, each on its own sheet of paper.

Identify inhibitors and deterrents. Study each specific goal and identify what might prevent you from achieving it. Write down those factors. This is not an exercise in pessimism; it is to help you remember that "the world" is probably not in 100% agreement with your goal. So consider both internal and external inhibitors and deterrents that could possibly interfere with you reaching your goal. Some examples might be: criticism by spouse, family, friends, or colleagues; personal impatience; running out of money; growing weary; coming to resent giving up something else in order to reach your goal.

Develop plans to cope with potential inhibitors and deterrents. This step needs to be done together with the previous step. It is necessary to build into your plan solutions to potential problems—how you will deal with and resolve them. This is where factors such as trade-off, delayed gratification, and sacrifice may come into play. Since time, energy, and money are probably not unlimited, consider what pursuing your goal will cost you. What will you have to surrender, postpone, or displace if you are to achieve your goal?

Specify measurements and develop a time line. Write out your goal in such a way that you can measure specifically your movement toward achieving it. Chart out a time line identifying specifically when you will have achieved the goal. Then determine how much of your goal you will have achieved at certain points in time along the way. Do this graphically on your goal sheet.

Build in reinforcers and supports along the way. For instance, plan some simple way to reward yourself for having successfully gotten your project off the ground and on its way. Celebrate having achieved your half-way mark, and so forth, on to the final achievement. Enlist a relative, friend, or colleague who may be available to provide support and encouragement along the way to your goal.

The process I have just described may sound like a rather mechanical treatment of something as personal and dynamic as realizing your capability. Perhaps. But I know it works, and I cannot overstate the importance of the establishment of specific goals and entering into sound planning.

Rule 3: Be realistic and recognize limitations.

Setting out to realize your capability is an exciting adventure; but as you do this there is the possibility of getting carried away in a sweep of unreality. We are neither unlimited nor omnipotent. We dare not let ourselves get caught up in the extravagance of believing there is nothing we cannot do or be. We are limited both by internal and external factors. *Sometimes* the old adages such as "Where there's a will, there's a way," and "Practice makes perfect," simply aren't true, and can in fact be detrimental. I am very fond of downhill skiing, and I love to watch the grace and skill of ski jumpers. However, because of the physical condition of my knees, ski jumping is beyond my capability. I covet being able to do it, I have plenty of will, and I'm willing to practice; but I also prefer to walk without crutches.

Age, muscular structure, and intelligence are some of the internal factors that demand we be realistic in setting goals. Socioeconomic status, prejudice, and societal values are some of the external factors. As you seek to realize your capability, be realistic in identifying the limitations to your capability.

Rule 4: Practice visualization.

Under Rule 1, I spoke about the need to believe in yourself and to exercise the power of positive expectation. If you wish to realize your capability you will "see" yourself realizing it; you will visualize your goal as having already been reached; you will experience internally the realization of your capability even as you are in process; and that internal experience will facilitate the actual achievement of your goal.

Ernest Holmes, in a small book entitled "The Golden Force," has provided a system for the "visualizing" dimension of realizing your capability. I had practiced this system quite naturally from my youth on, without knowing it. I knew the process had worked for me repeatedly, and I had shared it with many others. I was pleasantly surprised to read Holmes' presentation; I realized then that this process of visualization I had discovered for myself was an integral part of the experience of self-actualization.

Begin the process by picturing in your mind's eye what it is that you want to create and make manifest in your life. Visualize in fine detail the fulfillment of your goal. Be as inclusive and explicit as you can in your visualization. Lay everything else aside and focus your mind completely on this visualization. Be sure that you truly want and are going to accept the achievement of this goal, the realization of this aspect of your capability.

Offer this up as a prayer in accordance with the will of God. Have no question about whether it will be or not be. Always remember the generosity of the Creator. "You open your hand and satisfy the desires of every living thing" (Ps. 145:16). "Ask and it will be given to you; seek and you will find; knock and the door will be opened to you. For everyone who asks receives; he who seeks finds; and to him who knocks, the door will be opened" (Matt. 7:7-8). "If you believe, you will receive whatever you ask for in prayer" (Matt. 21:22).

Accept fully what you have chosen to do or be with an affirmation of, "It is here—it is happening." This process of visualization implants firmly in our unconscious the realization or actualization of the goal we have established. While we work externally *toward* the realization (which has already been fixed and accepted internally), our experience of life is influenced by the projection of that internal force. Plain and simply, we unconsciously influence the environment and set ourselves up to realize our goal, while we are at the same time working consciously to realize it.

Rule 5. Avoid procrastination.
Procrastination is not necessarily the result of laziness; nor is it usually merely a bad habit. More often

than not it involves issues of self-esteem, fear of failure, and fear of success. We have already treated the issue of self-esteem in Rule 1 and Key Number 1. In Rules 6 and 7 we will deal with fear of failure and fear of success.

Procrastination is simply to put things off habitually. Perfectionism becomes the norm for the person of low self-esteem. Fear of not being able to attain the "perfect" causes people to do nothing—to put things off.

Rule 6. Accept failure.

Abraham Lincoln may be an exceptional case, but he is an outstanding example of realizing his capability in spite of failure. Consider his track record:

1831—Failed in business

1836—Experienced an emotional breakdown

1838—Was defeated for speaker of the house

1848—Lost renomination to Congress

1849—Rejected for land officer

1850—Defeated for Senate

1856—Lost nomination for vice president

1858—Defeated for Senate

1860—Elected president

Thomas Edison's school teacher called him a dunce. He is reported to have failed in 14,000 attempts before he perfected the first electric light bulb.

Both Albert Einstein and Werner von Braun flunked math courses.

Enrico Caruso failed so many times with his high notes that his voice teacher advised him to give it up. Caruso did not. Instead he became one of the greatest tenors of all time.

A few years ago the *Wall Street Journal* carried a feature article with the headline, "Taking Chances: How Four Companies Spawn New Products By Encouraging Risks; Failures Are Part of the Game." The lead paragraphs of the article told about 3M's fiasco in manufacturing a woman's brassiere. Very few people ever heard about the 3M brassiere because the company's first order was also its last. A failure? Absolutely. But not the end of the story.

Following the fiasco, 3M researchers continued to experiment with the special bra fabric and came up with a variation on the material that was particularly suitable for surgical masks and ultimately for industrial safety masks. "From bust to dust" was the inside joke to describe the fascinating history of 3M's occupational health and safety products division, which recorded more than $25 million in sales per year at the beginning of this decade.

Failure will not prevent you from realizing your capability. The fear of failure will.

I noted in Rule 5 that the fear of failure is a root of procrastination. That fear can keep you much too close to the slothful, vagrant end of this continuum even though you may very well *not* be slothful or vagrant.

Despite the countless illustrations that indicate how failure is normal and even show the positive potential of it, there still persists in our society the attitude that it is inappropriate to fail. It is as if there were an eleventh commandment: "Thou shalt not fail."

There are too many potentially positive results of failure to allow the fear of it to prevent your realizing your capability. Let me list some of them:

● Failure can show you the limits of your capability. For example, high jumpers never discover their full potential until they reach their failure point.

● Failure can help you identify your strengths and weaknesses.

● Failure can tell you what you can and cannot do. It is quite unrealistic to expect to be able to do everything and do it well.

● Repeated failure can tell you that you might be wise to lay one thing aside and expend your energy on another endeavor.

● Failure is an event, not a person. You may fail, but *you* are not a failure.

● Failure can generate creativity.

Accept failure as part of the normal experience of life. Accept the fact that failure can actually be helpful to you as you work to realize your capability and strive to become an imperfect achiever.

The world of sports is fascinating in that we watch athletes who are indeed achievers (some of great renown) who nevertheless demonstrate considerable imperfection. They are hardly slothful, but neither, on the other hand, would I call them workaholics, perfectionists, or compulsives. They seem to have found a fulfilling blend of these opposites and a comfortable midpoint between these extremes of the continuum.

Professional baseball players with the greatest number of home runs usually also log the greatest number of strikeouts.

Rule 7. Don't be afraid of success.

There is a certain irony here associated with realizing your capability. It is not too difficult to understand procrastination that comes from fear of failure. "I hesitate to try to realize my capability because I am afraid

I would fail." But it may be very hard to understand why a person would hesitate out of the fear that he or she might succeed. Why would people be afraid of actually achieving the very thing for which they are striving? Why would they actually sabotage their own success?

Andy had worked for a large institution for 18 years. For six years he functioned successfully as the vice president, all the while hopefully eyeing the number one position. Finally the boss retired and Andy was given the top job. Within a week of his appointment he tried to take his life. Only after his attempted suicide did his anxieties surface and his fear of success become obvious.

In Andy's growing-up experience he had developed a problem of dependency because of an overprotective mother. He became a rather meek and submissive person, and later, in the world of work, achieved advancement through his quiet, diligent performance. Ultimately, though, Andy could not allow other people to depend on him, and as president, that could not be avoided. Furthermore, Andy feared some form of retaliation from subordinates because he had risen above them.

Beth was employed by a large brokerage house where her chance for advancement was almost unlimited. She had successfully graduated from college and from graduate school. Soon after she landed the job at the brokerage house she was titled a "Wall Street whiz kid." Her superiors unabashedly told her, "You're the best employee who has ever come through here." Beth accepted the praise politely but became so anxious she had to go home. She continued to go to work, but could no longer perform as she had.

Beth's experience of success unleashed a barrage of guilt and fear. She had grown up in a family of few means and was the only person in the family to complete college and graduate school. The family had only one book in the house—the Bible. Beth's father had consistently expressed contempt for book learning and Beth was afraid that because of her academic achievement her father would focus his hostility on her.

Fortunately there are happy endings to the stories of Andy and Beth because professionals were able to help them abandon their fear of success. But Andy and Beth are not unique. The issues in their lives are perhaps a little more prominent than among some others of us, but the fear of success is entirely too real to too many people who want to realize their capability.

Rule 8. Study the traits of self-fulfilled people.

What follows is a partial list of the wide variety of characteristics of people who are self-fulfilled and who realize their capability.

● They are happy with their choice of vocation. They don't envy people in other positions or wish they had chosen a different field of endeavor.

● They are spontaneous, with a "naturalness" about them.

● They are competitive.

● They are autonomous; they have taken charge of their lives.

● They are social extraverts but not without the quality of detachment and the enjoyment of privacy.

● They enjoy work and believe in the work ethic. They generally maintain that you can start with nothing and work your way to the top.

● They are pragmatic; they use what works. They are not influenced by prejudices or preconceived ideas.

● They believe fortune smiles on them and never see themselves as unlucky.

● They perceive reality clearly and are comfortable with it.

● They often rely on intuition in problem solving. They study a problem, consider the facts, examine alternatives, and conclude, "I have a hunch this is the way to go."

● They seek variety and avoid routine.

● They are accepting of themselves, others, and the world.

Rule 9. Understand the temptations of workaholism.

Only a small percentage of work addicts or workaholics are "people who simply like to work a lot." There are such people; their work is their life, their whole being. But the great majority of people caught up in workaholism, perfectionism, and compulsiveness are there because of a wide variety of reasons other than that. Workaholism is a very tempting mask to cover a multitude of problems, dynamics, issues, and illnesses. Here is a partial listing of the backgrounds of workaholism, perfectionism, and compulsiveness:

Problems with self-image and self-esteem head the list. Overachievers are often overcompensating for a poor self-image, trying to prove to the world that they are persons of worth and value. In our performance-oriented society, productivity, ability, and self-worth are interrelated. "My worth as a person is determined by my ability, and my ability is determined by what I produce. Therefore, the more I produce, the more I am worth." Typically, such people feel like nobodies away from work; consequently the temptation to workaholism is enormous.

Escape from failure or potential failure entices people into perfectionism and compulsiveness. If I am perfect or compulsively cover all my bases, no one can ever accuse me of failure.

Some people are tempted into workaholism to meet their need for respect, recognition, and praise. Art grew up in poverty in the slums of a large city. As a boy he was ashamed even to tell people where he lived. Today he is a successful professional who works long hours and is deeply involved simultaneously in half a dozen projects at all times. The achievement of work is Art's way of proving himself to the world.

Fear of intimacy is another root of workaholism. People who don't want people to get too close, or who are afraid of being intimate themselves with others, may retreat into workaholism—which simply doesn't allow time for such closeness. Some people even fear being alone with themselves and must have an almost constant involvement of activity.

Greed or the accumulation of "this world's goods" can be fulfilled by workaholism. I saw a T-shirt which said, "He who dies with the most toys, wins." More than likely, he who dies with the most toys, dies with nothing else.

Workaholism may be a pitch for sympathy. This connection is related to a poor self-image. "Don't you feel sorry for me because of all the work I must do?" "Because of all the work I must do I can't do this and have no time for that. Pity poor me."

One extreme of this continuum may be a response to fearing the other extreme. Some people are workaholics because they think they are actually lazy. They work as long and hard as they do because they fear their innate sloth will otherwise take over.

Guilt. Workaholism, perfectionism, and compulsiveness may be a form of self-punishment or atonement for feelings of guilt (rational or irrational). The workaholism is then fueled by the drive to "make up" for the crime.

Workaholism, perfectionism, and compulsiveness are detrimental to wellness because essentially they seek to deny humanity. They are tempting because they appear to "resolve" many social, psychological, and spiritual issues for us. That is their seduction. Not only do they fail to resolve, they make us exceedingly vulnerable. Workaholism, perfectionism, and compulsiveness generate stress and stress depletes our immune system. The common virus fighter *immunoglobulin-A* found in human saliva was shown in experiments to be markedly decreased in production when subjects were under stress. Perhaps we need a new bumper sticker which says:

BE WELL!
ACCEPT HUMAN IMPERFECTION!
Your own and others.

Rule 10: Act!

The film *Chariots of Fire* was essentially a true story. It focused on two runners who were determined to win, Harold Abrahams and Eric Liddell. Both won gold medals at the 1924 Paris Olympics. At one point in the film, Abrahams lost a race to Liddell and was terribly discouraged. He wanted to quit. He cried out to his friend, "I run to win. If I don't win, I don't run." To which his friend angrily replied, "And if you don't run, you won't win."

He ran again and he won.

To realize your capability you must act. There is no other way. As in the process of visualization, we "see" the achievement, the actualization, and the realization of a goal, and *know* it is ours; but we must act to *make* it ours. In the opening verses of the Old Testament book of Joshua, we hear God say essentially this very thing to Joshua: "Now it is for you to cross the Jordan, you and this whole people of Israel, to the land which I am giving them. Every place where you set foot is yours: I have given it to you, as I promised Moses" (Josh. 1:2-3 NEB).

And so we "possess" what is already ours as we realize our capability. We use the gifts we have been given and feel the satisfaction of fulfillment.

Key Number 6

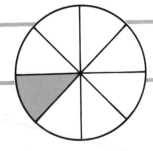

Express Your Feelings

Finding your path between suppression and impulsiveness.

*I*n my work as a chaplain and counselor, I try to help people identify and come to terms with their feelings. Frequently I show people a list of 150 "feeling words" to help them describe how they feel:

Q. How do you feel about that?

A. I feel abandoned
       adequate
       affected
       afraid
       aggravated
       alienated
       ambivalent
       angry
       annoyed
       antsy
       anxious

apathetic
appreciative
apprehensive
ashamed
astonished
awful
awkward
bewildered
bewitched
bitter
bored

bothered
bugged
burdened
carefree
captivated
cautious
cheated
cheered
cold
comfortable
comforted

concerned
condemned
confident
content
cowardly
daring
deflated
delighted
depressed
deprived
despondent
destructive
devilish
disappointed
discontented
disgraced
disgusted
displeased
distraught
distressed
disturbed
distrustful
doubtful
duped
eager
ecstatic
elated
embarrassed
enchanted
encouraged
envious
excited
fascinated
fed up
foolish

forlorn
frightened
frustrated
giddy
glad
glorious
grateful
grieved
guilty
happy
harassed
harried
hassled
hesitant
honored
hopeful
hopeless
humiliated
hurt
ignored
impatient
impressed
inadequate
indifferent
irritated
jealous
joyful
jubilant
left out
lonely
lost
miserable
morbid
nervous
overjoyed

overwhelmed
overwrought
pained
playful
pleased
proud
provoked
put down
put out
put upon
rageful
rash
reassured
refreshed
rejected
relieved
resentful
resigned
robbed
sad
satisfied
scared
shaken up
silly
soothed
strained
stupid
surprised
tense
terrible
trapped
turned off
turned on
unburdened
uncertain

uncomfortable	vengeful	witty
uneasy	vulnerable	worried
unsure	warm	wretched
upset	weary	wrought up

Some people have trouble with the concept of feelings. Others have difficulty identifying feelings. Still others find it hard to put their feelings into words.

The Effect of Feelings on Our State of Health

Feelings are friends and feelings are foes. We experience good feelings and not-so-good feelings. They are an integral part of all our lives and have a significant influence on our overall state of health.

Sometimes the terms *emotions* and *feelings* are used interchangeably. Strictly speaking, *emotions* are identified as the biophysiological state (including the chemical changes) which underlies the sensations we experience. *Feelings* are identified as the subjective awareness of that emotional state.

Over a hundred years ago William James defined *emotion* as "a state of mind that manifests itself by sensible changes in the body." With every emotion, changes take place in muscles, blood vessels, viscera, and endocrine glands. The subjective experience that accompanies this is the feeling.

To show the close relationship between emotion and our biophysiology, think of the external and internal signs of anger. Dr. W. B. Cannon of Harvard University studied them in detail and noted the following:[4]

EXTERNAL—

- Reddening of the skin of the face.
- Widening of the eyelids.
- Bloodshot whites of the eyes.
- Contraction and tightening of the lips.
- A setting of the jaw.
- Clenching of the fists.
- Tremor in the arms.
- Tremor in the voice.

INTERNAL—

- Blood immediately clots much more quickly than normal. (In anger, one may get into physical combat, suffer a wound, and bleed. The quick blood clotting is the body's safety measure.)
- The number of blood cells in the circulating blood increases substantially.
- The muscles at the outlet of the stomach squeeze down so tightly that nothing leaves the stomach.
- The entire digestive tract becomes so spastic that many people have severe abdominal pains during or after strong anger. (We refer to our stomach as being "all knotted up.")
- Heart rate increases, often to 180 or 220 beats per minute.
- Blood pressure rises markedly from a normal 130 to 230 or even higher. (A person may suffer a stroke in a fit of anger because the elevation of blood pressure caused the rupture of a blood vessel in the brain.)
- The coronary arteries in the heart squeeze down (often hard enough to produce angina pectoris, or even a coronary occlusion).

Even a quick review of this list indicates that it should not be too difficult to understand why people who are in a regular state of anger, or who carry with them repressed and unresolved anger, may easily develop coronary or gastrointestinal problems.

The importance of expressing your feelings is clear because emotions and feelings (both good and not-so-good) are an integral part of our lives and are as natural to us as breathing. We hear a funny story and we laugh. We receive bad news and we grieve. We receive good news and we rejoice. Someone abuses us and we are angry. Without feelings we are inhuman. To deny our feelings is to deny our humanity. To deny our humanity means we must become superhuman. That alone can generate considerable mental conflict because it means we no longer accept ourselves.

Feeling good is directly related to the appropriate expression of feelings. Recognizing, accepting, and appropriately expressing a feeling by dealing with it openly and talking it out discharges the physical and mental dynamics of it, and we are thus free to move on without residual effects.

Denying that a feeling exists or holding it in tends to retain the physical and mental charge of the emotion. When I experience anger, the physical and mental effects of it exist in reality and do not disappear simply because I say I am not angry. When I experience bitter disappointment, the physical and mental effects of it do not disappear simply because I say I am not disappointed. I may actually *believe* I am not angry or disappointed, but that is neither here nor there as far as the effects of the emotion on my body and mind are concerned. Feelings do not simply dissipate. Unless they are dealt with, their energy remains and accumulates with the energies of other denied or repressed feelings, thus presenting a very real threat to my overall health. It is not at all uncommon for them to cause actual physical breakdown (Emotionally Induced Illness) or mental dysfunction.

In spite of this, many people are reluctant to express their feelings, and instead either consciously suppress or unconsciously repress or deny them. For a variety of reasons many people remain close to the nonexpressive extreme of this continuum. Why should this be?

Five Reasons Why People Do Not Express Their Feelings (and What Can Be Done about Each One)

(1) The influence of home and family. I have already pointed out the significance of our childhood impressions in the process of growing up. This is particularly true in our expression or nonexpression of feelings. Most of us begin to learn very early in life that there are advantages to suppressing feelings rather than openly expressing them.

For many years my colleagues and I provided a five week course to help young people prepare for marriage. Our clients were mostly university students and others training for professional careers. One session in the course was entitled "Masculinity/Femininity," and was begun by our listing traits of each on a chalkboard. We would ask the attendees simply to call out words or short phrases which in their opinion were descriptive of masculinity and femininity, and we wrote them on the board.

When we finished, and the group had an opportunity to look carefully at its collective description of masculinity and femininity, a groan would inevitably rise from the group. "Did we say that! We didn't say that! You set us up! That's an ancient image!" Invariably these groups would construct a description of masculinity that was stereotypically machismo and a description of femininity that was stereotypically demure. Despite the fact that these were highly educated, intelligent, young people who complained that they "knew better than that," their responses still followed "ancient images."

The issue here is that there is a strong possibility of perpetuating old stereotypes even in the midst of the conscious desire to abandon them for more enlightened understanding. If the old stereotypes of male machismo and female coyness and dependency are resident in mommy and daddy, Jimmy will grow up firmly believing that "Big boys don't cry," and Jane will grow up firmly believing that assertiveness is not for "nice" girls. Suppression and repression of feelings will continue to be the order of the day.

Men cry only 20% as often as women—which may partly explain why they are more prone to stress-related illnesses.

Parents are our primary models. Much of what we learn as we grow up is learned by observing them. If they do not express their feelings, and if we want to emulate them (as do most children), this will simply add to the case for suppressing and repressing feelings. Further, if you reveal yourself and your feelings and are put down, censured, or somehow invalidated, chances are you won't do it again. For instance, if you were reprimanded or physically struck when you expressed anger, you would develop a strong tendency to suppress and then repress angry feelings. Likewise, if you were told to "Quit moping around and get busy" when you demonstrated feelings of disappointment and despondency, you would probably mature into an adult who denies feelings of despair and smiles through *all* of life's experiences.

Parents who do not demonstrate affection to each other and appropriate affection to their children teach their children that the public expression of loving feelings is inappropriate and is reserved for the marriage bed—if even there. They echo society in general and declare, "You just don't do that. What would people say?"

In Key Number 1, I dealt with the issue of the influence of home and family on the development of self-image. Much of the directive for coping with that (especially Step 7) is applicable here. You realize now that it is not "wrong," but in fact beneficial to you to express your feelings rather than to repress them. At one time you sincerely believed that repressing them was the thing to do. Now you *know better*. Leave that old baggage behind and move on.

(2) The influence of society in general and religious institutions in particular. Generally speaking, society prefers the status quo. Society likes solid, calm, smooth, predictable experience. Aside from notable exceptions deemed acceptable and in fact commendable, society does not appreciate the public display of emotion. Society has its taboos, and if you violate them

you will be properly punished. Mild violations bring such "punishments" as frowns, raised eyebrows, eyes rolled back in the head, and being ignored by observers who pretend they did not see what they saw. More severe violations bring punishments ranging up to severe fines and imprisonment.

Two of the notable exceptions to this are sports events (especially contact sports) and the death of a "great person." Spectators at a sports event are expected to express a great range of feelings, from the pits of despair ("Those clumsy dogs!") to adulation and ecstasy ("We're the greatest!") to blatant rage ("Kill that _____ !")

At the death of a "great person," society lifts its ban on the public shedding of tears and allows all (even military *men*) to weep without recrimination.

Elsewhere, if you publicly express feelings of anger, someone is bound to let you know you need to "cool it" and practice better self-control. If you shout and jump up and down because you are feeling great joy and exultation, someone is sure to tell you you ought to "settle down." If you feel sadness and grief and express it by crying, someone will inevitably encourage you to "pull yourself together."

Religious institutions have often encouraged the suppression of natural feelings. Christians have been told that they are supposed to be peaceful; therefore the expression of anger is out of place. In fact, they should not even *have* the feeling of anger. They have been told that they should never experience doubts or questions; consequently they should not express feelings of anxiety and uncertainty. When loved ones have died, they have been told not to weep and grieve their loss but to continue on in "strength" so that they will be an example to others to do likewise. They have been told never to experience disappointment or despondency; therefore they are not to express feelings of despair.

The expectations of society, be they actual or perceived expectations, are a potent influence on whether we express or suppress our feelings. This influence must, however, always be balanced against the non-healthful dimension of suppression and denial of feelings. Appropriate expression is the solution to the dilemma.

When you realize that it is truly not "wrong" to express your feelings, you will be motivated to do it. You will leave those old inhibitors behind and move on.

(3) The need for a strong persona. In Key Number 4, I described *persona* as a sort of mask we wear as we present ourselves to society. It is the image we present in public life. Of course those images vary from person to person and within the same person from time to time, depending largely on how you think you should present yourself. There is invariably a dimension of inauthenticity about persona, but that is required in a civilized culture. It becomes problematic only when the persona becomes too thick or too greatly alienated from the person you perceive yourself to be.

Mary sat in my office talking with me about her husband who had died just one and a half hours earlier. She was an intelligent, educated, well-dressed, sophisticated woman whom I believe had loved her husband dearly, but who also believed that crying was beneath her dignity. "Crying is acceptable, perhaps helpful for others," she said, "but I believe I should be above it. I know it is a release, but it is a rather undesirable display of emotion."

Mary liked to believe that she presented the persona of a strong person, which indeed she did. Therefore she was convinced that she had to be "above" crying. To her, crying would damage her image.

The pains of "professional persona." "People in my position need to be stoic," a man once said to me. "It would be a severe loss of face, a real embarrassment, for me to get emotional in public." He was a man suffering from what I call the pains of "professional persona."

Virtually every vocation has its stereotyped image, which may or may not allow for the expression of feelings. The man who told me that he needed to be stoic was in a position of leadership in a large corporation. He believed that if he were ever to display emotion publicly he would lose credibility in his position, and quite possibly, ultimately lose his position. I have experienced the pains of professional persona many times in my career. Not because I suppressed feelings that were "inappropriate" to the stereotype of my profession, but because I expressed them.

For several years I worked as the pastor of a church in Maryland. Over the years I enjoyed a warm and close relationship with the people of that congregation. When our third child was born and then died just three days after birth, our family was grief-stricken. Our son's death occurred on a Sunday morning, and because of circumstances I had no opportunity to relate any of the story to the congregation. I knew they wanted to know what had happened, so the following Sunday I told the story very briefly during the time for announcements in the worship service. My voice broke and I had to stop momentarily for my tears more than once, but I told the story and then went on to complete the service. After the service, I stood at the door greeting people as they left. I noticed one of the men had waited behind to be the last one out of church. I suspected he might have some special feelings to talk about. He did, but it wasn't what I expected. When everyone else was outside the doors he said to me, "Reverend, if *you* can't keep it together, how do you think *we* can?"

The need for a strong persona may quite effectively inhibit the expression of feelings. However, there may be an error in thinking that a strong persona is necessary. You need to determine if the maintenance of a strong image is worth the price of suppressing and denying natural feelings. In my opinion, it is not.

People who suppress tears may be more likely to develop colitis and ulcers.

---

(4) The need for control. The need to appear "in charge" and "on top of things" all the time will successfully disallow the natural expression of feelings. If you fear the consequences (whatever you perceive them to be) of not appearing to be in control at all times, you will not allow yourself to express normal feelings. Some people fear ridicule from others if they express feelings because they have been taught that being open is a sign of weakness. Many of my counselees have experienced embarrassment when they wept in the privacy of my office. As we talk and explore together, they often become aware of many new feelings. Some of those feelings evoke tears. Almost

invariably, even in the intimacy of a counseling relationship, whether man or woman, the person will apologize with words like, "I'm so sorry, I didn't mean to do this," or "I really shouldn't cry like this."

Helen was a patient in a psychiatric treatment program. Upon admission she was severely depressed. In the course of her treatment we discovered that she had never worked through the grief of the death of her husband *many* years ago. Her husband died one week after the assassination of President Kennedy. Helen had watched with a kind of admiration how "the widow Kennedy held up so bravely" in the public telecasts of the events following the president's death. When her own husband died just shortly after Kennedy's burial, Helen declared, "If Jackie Kennedy can do it, so can I." Here now, a great many years later, Helen, who had denied and repressed her manifold feelings of grief because of her need to be in control, was finally allowing herself to express them.

Being in control and being on top of everything all the time is terribly demanding of any human being. The joy of feeling good requires a surrender to our humanity—we cannot expect to live above it. Instead we will break down physically or mentally. The solution is to let go of that strong need and risk the natural expression of normal human feelings.

(5) The need to be a caretaker or protector. In Key Number 3, I described the overcaring personality. Such an overcaring attitude will also encourage the suppression and denial of feelings. The overcaring person says, "I don't want to hurt her feelings by expressing mine. I don't want to upset her by telling her how angry I am or how sad and disappointed I am

about her behavior." This is nothing more or less than enabler language. The enabler thus "stuffs" his or her own feelings and continues to take care of the other person.

The suppression and repression of feelings for the supposed purpose of protecting the other person is similar. "He is too weak. He couldn't stand my expression of feelings. He has enough of his own 'stuff' to bear. I don't want to burden him with more than he can handle."

Such caretaker's comments as these are frankly flimsy rationalizations for not expressing one's feelings. Here no one gains—all parties lose. Those who are being protected lose because they are allowed to continue on without being confronted with the feelings that their behavior is generating in the lives of others. Those protecting lose because they must continue to suppress feelings which need to be expressed for the sake of themselves as well as others. Recognizing the fact that all parties lose should be sufficient to discourage such caretaking and protecting and to encourage appropriate expression of feelings.

Three Steps to Expressing Feelings: Accept—Identify—Speak

(1) Accept the reasonableness, healthiness, and inevitability of feelings. This first step is *fundamental* because of the existence of the five reasons above and all the other reasons why people do not express their feelings. It is important to know that:

• feelings are essentially the awareness we have of the emotions we experience in our daily living.

● feelings are going to happen to you just as surely as you are human. Unless you are a severely psychopathic personality, you will have feelings.

● you will experience feelings if you simply allow them to happen. In most cases people do not have to *learn* to express feelings—they simply need to stop squelching them.

● feelings are not bad or evil or to be feared and thus suppressed, repressed, or denied.

● the Creator has created us to be feeling people. This is part of the beauty and brilliance of our creation.

If we accept the fact that life is full of situations, experiences, events, and people that naturally generate the whole spectrum of feelings within us, we can be free of guilt or fear in expressing our feelings and no longer need to suppress or repress them. We are *allowed* to fear, allowed to grieve, allowed to rejoice and celebrate, allowed to be angry, and allowed to doubt.

(2) Become aware of your feelings and identify them. Once you are convinced that it is all right to have feelings, the next step is to become aware of your feelings and identify them. This may appear to be a rather obvious step, but for people who have been in the habit of suppressing and denying feelings it requires conscious effort.

Jerry was the pastor of a small congregation in the Great Plains. To supplement his income he raised a few head of cattle. One Friday before leaving to go back to his home for the weekend, Jerry told me about a deal he had struck with a fellow to sell him two head of cattle. He was going to close the deal the following day. On Monday, when Jerry came in, he appeared depressed. When I asked him if something was wrong, he told me about the sale of the cattle and how the fellow had swindled him in the deal. As he recounted the story he became very animated, agitated, and then more and more angry. He demonstrated virtually all the external symptoms of anger which I listed at the beginning of this chapter. As he wound up his story I said, "Wow, that was really infuriating, wasn't it?"

Jerry replied, "No, I'm not angry—I'm upset."

An objective observer could rightfully comment that Jerry's statement was absurd. But it was true—for Jerry. He had been taught and truly believed that clergy should not be angry. They should set an example of always being calm and peaceful. So despite the fact that he demonstrated a host of clear signs of anger (even mild rage), Jerry did not identify his feeling as that of anger.

Dr. Willard Gaylin, in his book *Feelings: Our Vital Signs,* tells of a patient who, when demonstrably angry, felt a unique kind of internal "pressure" of the most unpleasant kind, which he assumed to be some form of abdominal spasm. He could not "honestly say that it was painful." It was more like "gnawing and unpleasant." "It is something akin to hunger," he once said.

Many people simply have never learned to tune in on, "get in touch with," and identify the language of feelings. The partial list of feeling words at the beginning of this chapter contains base-line feeling words such as *angry, cheated, depressed, embarrassed, frightened, happy, joyful,* etc., as well as more subtle words and nuances of these base-line words such as *bugged, duped, despondent, playful,* etc. The list includes good feeling words and not-so-good feeling words. Study them, review them, repeat them aloud, and look them up in the dictionary if they're unfamiliar. Try to visualize an experience where you would feel each feeling.

Throughout the day, when you are experiencing an emotion, take the list of feeling words and try to pinpoint the word that best describes what you are feeling. Take time to write down the feeling word, plus what you can describe about what was going on within you as you experienced the feeling, as well as the setting (occasion, place, event) in which it occurred. Here's an illustration:

"It was shortly after lunch when my boss stopped at my desk, handed me some papers, and said, 'Marty, we need some figures on this job for a meeting tomorrow at 8:30. Get a pretty firm estimate worked up, will you please, so I can have it by 8:00 tomorrow morning.'

"I got warm, even a little sweaty. I noticed I was a little short of breath. I got up and got a drink of water. I came back to my desk and looked over the feeling word list. The one that seemed to describe what was going on was 'overwhelmed.' I also think there was something like 'put upon' and 'angry' there too."

Next in the process, spend about 15 minutes sometime later in the day talking about your notes on your feelings. Do this with your spouse or an interested friend. This way you will have an opportunity to *speak* about your written work, and that will help you gain even more insight into your feelings. Such continued practice will help you to become much more aware of what you are feeling and to identify it clearly in words.

Incidentally, be cautious when identifying the feeling of anger. There is usually something more involved. Anger is often a secondary feeling. That means it is the result of another feeling. Some of the primary feelings leading into anger are hurt and disappointment, fear, embarrassment, frustration, helplessness, and feeling put down.

(3) Speak your feelings and act them out appropriately. When Paul wrote his letter to the Ephesian Christians, giving them guidelines to live by, he wisely advised, "Be angry but do not sin; do not let the sun go down on your anger" (Eph. 4:26 RSV). I take that to mean that he realized anger is an inevitable human experience. So much for Step 1. He recognized that one experiencing and identifying anger (Step 2) would find it necessary to express it appropriately (Step 3). But what is "appropriately"? The answer is: in a manner without deliberate intent to harm others or oneself. Furthermore, he encouraged the Ephesians to express anger appropriately, in a timely fashion. This means at the time when it is experienced or very shortly thereafter. It is not to be held overnight or longer. It is not to be suppressed or repressed, for there it can fester and possibly grow into deep resentment or even vengeful desire. Remember, simply ignoring anger does not make it go away.

Impulsive and spontaneous expression of feelings. In order to express feelings appropriately, that is, without deliberate intent to harm, I believe it is helpful to distinguish between impulsive and spontaneous expression. Both approaches satisfy the need to express feelings, but spontaneity possesses a kind of "proprietary control" which is absent in impulsiveness. In spontaneous expression the person is more in charge of the feeling and guides its expression. In impulsive expression something of the opposite seems to be true—the feeling itself in its emotional charge is in control and guides the person in acting it out. Impulsive expression seems to bypass or knock down personal and societal filters and governors as well as the rules and guidelines of common sense, good manners, and social graces. Spontaneous expression, on the other hand, is likewise free and uninhibited, unpremeditated and voluntary, but with consideration for the very filters and governors, guidelines, and common sense that impulsive expression disregards. Impulsive expression is "me-centered." Spontaneous expression is considerate of others.

Impulsive expression of feelings is simply more base and uncontrolled, liking to act out raw feelings without any refinement. We have all experienced these urges in varying degrees and know their potential danger.

Most of us have had the experience of receiving unwanted phone calls from companies that try to increase their business through telemarketing. Frequently these callers ask quite personal questions about our families and finances. I remember one such occasion when I became very irritated and told the caller that the answers to her questions were none of her business.

In retrospect, I wasn't too pleased with my behavior. I could have been much more appropriate and better mannered, but instead I let my anger impulsively blurt out. And I was sorry I had done it.

Impulsive acting out of raw feelings of greater degree than this can become destructive. Verbal, physical, and sexual abuse may all arise out of impulsive expression of raw feelings. Impulsive people simply "let fly" their feelings, negative as well as positive, with little or no regard for the surroundings of the situation or the consequences of their behavior.

Spontaneous expression of feelings is appropriate.
Spontaneous expression of feelings, on the other hand,
honors the guidelines of socially acceptable behavior.
It, too, is free and uninhibited. Spontaneity does not
enter a punched card into the psyche's computer of
propriety and then get a printout (so to speak) directing
the expression. Such an expression of feelings would
hardly be spontaneous.

Perhaps a comparison would help. Let's say that
spouses Alice and David have a joint checking account.
Alice's record keeping has been an issue with David
for some time because she has not been noting in the
checkbook the amounts of checks written, and has also
been careless in her addition and subtraction. For two
consecutive months David has pointed out Alice's care-
lessness and has asked her to be more careful and
deliberate. Each time Alice agreed. Now they have
just received the monthly bank statement, which David
carefully studies. Soon he becomes agitated and gets
up from the table, taking the statement and cancelled
checks with him. He goes over to where Alice is seat-
ed. What follows in the scenario is described on the
next page.

Both of the forms described on page 143 allow David to express his feeling of anger. However, there will
be a marked difference in his relationship with Alice
as a result of the two different expressions of anger.
The impulsive expression is destructive because it hu-
miliates, blames, and judges Alice. David projects responsibility for his feelings onto Alice. Alice's response is bound to be defensive. Good communication
is virtually shut off. David's impulsive expression of
anger can seriously hurt Alice and their relationship.

IMPULSIVE	SPONTANEOUS
David throws down the statement and cancelled checks in front of Alice. Alice is startled, looking up to see the cancelled checks fluttering down around her and David's face taunt with anger. David says in deliberate tones, "I am sick and tired of having to clean up after you. You're an irresponsible and sloppy bookkeeper. You can't even add two and two and get four."	David lays out the check-book before Alice and says to her, "I want you to know that I am really angry because you consistently forget to enter the amounts of checks you have written, and you regularly make mistakes in this checkbook because you don't take the time to check your arithmetic. That means that I have to spend at least an hour every month when the bank statement arrives, trying to locate the errors and reconcile the account."

In the spontaneous expression of anger, David admits to his feeling of anger and clearly reports to Alice his response to what she has done and how it has affected him. David's stance, voice, and facial expression are consistent with his words and Alice gets the message. The encounter is healthy; the channel for communication between David and Alice is left open and there is a good possibility that the issues can be resolved.

Have you expressed anger inappropriately? Apologize, admit your mistake, and ask forgiveness.

Four Benefits
of Expressing Feelings

Here are four major benefits that come from the spontaneous expression of feelings:

(1) Freedom from the burden of suppressed or repressed feelings. Carrying suppressed (those you know about) and repressed (those you don't know about) feelings around requires a lot of psychic energy. Expressing feelings in the here and now frees up that energy for creative purposes. Also, the likelihood of emotionally-induced illness, prompted by denial and repressed feelings, is significantly decreased.

(2) Greater personal authenticity. It is a joyous feeling to be able to assert yourself by appropriately expressing your feelings. You become more genuine. You "beat around the bush" less and play fewer "games" such as passive aggression instead of direct, open, and honest expression.

(3) Improvement in communication. Consider again the illustration of Alice and David. While there is indeed a risk involved in David's spontaneous expression of anger, there is the greater possibility of open communication about the issue and how it might be solved. As a result of the confrontation, David and Alice may in fact come even closer together in their relationship because the expression of feeling was done in love, without bitterness or judgment.

Suppose, however, that David does not spontaneously express his feeling of anger to Alice, but instead suppresses it (which, incidentally, is so often the case). The result would be nothing less than resentment and the bearing of a grudge which would only grow and fester inside David. Alice would know nothing of his anger and would only continue on in her "error." The result of David's unexpressed anger would be a passive-aggressive "getting even" with Alice, or an ultimate "explosion" by David that could seriously damage their relationship.

(4) Greater potential for intimacy and empathy. Being a "closed" person is an effective defense; it protects you from people getting close to you. Being "open" leaves you vulnerable to being hurt, but available for intimacy with others. Empathy is the wonderful ability to move into the skin of another person and experience the world through his or her eyes and ears. Being open and expressive of yourself allows you to be more empathic with others. We human beings need each other.

Key Number 7

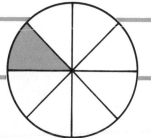

Practice Your Faith

Finding your path between overdependence and independence.

*T*he year was 1931. A young man, wealthy and talented, traveled from America to Zurich, Switzerland, to place himself under the care of Dr. Carl G. Jung, a physician who was later to be identified as one of the founders of modern psychiatry. The young man had found himself on the brink of despair over his uncontrollable drinking and his previous failures at attempted "cures." He spent nearly a year with Jung, then left treatment with great respect for the doctor and much confidence in his new self.

However, the young man quickly relapsed into intoxication. Still, he was convinced that Jung was his salvation. He returned to Zurich and remained in Jung's care until the psychiatrist finally told him frankly that his condition was medically and psychiatrically hopeless. His only hope, said Jung, lay in his undergoing a transforming experience of the spirit.

Over a period of a couple years and through a fascinating series of events, Jung's message to the young man was communicated to a man named Bill Wilson, who was in extremely severe circumstances due to his desperate alcoholism. In time, Wilson had a "transformation of the spirit," and he never had another drink. Shortly afterward, he met Dr. Bob Smith, who in time also sobered up and together with Wilson founded Alcoholics Anonymous. Wilson later wrote to Jung and credited him for his significant part in giving the program of Alcoholics Anonymous its spiritual undergirding.

Throughout his practice of medicine, Jung was sensitive to the element of spirituality in the lives of people. He wrote, "Among all my patients in the second half of life—that is to say, over thirty-five—there has not been one whose problem in the last resort was not that of finding a religious outlook on life. It is safe to say that every one of them fell ill because he had lost that which the living religions of every age have given to their followers, and none of them has been really healed who did not regain his religious outlook."[5]

The Presence of the Spiritual Dimension

What was Jung talking about? What is the significance of a person's spirituality to feeling good? Was he suggesting that one cannot truly be healed without the active involvement of his or her spiritual dimension?

We alone of all creatures are created in the image of God. It is the presence of the Spirit of God within us that makes us unique. Regardless of how we identify it, or choose to call it, or *not* call it, our spiritual dimension is there and available to us, just as are the other dimensions of human life.

My practice of ministry has confirmed for me Jung's observation. It has become clear to me that there is a high correlation between the depth of the positive spiritual dimension of a person's life and that person's ability to succeed in passing through stresses and crises. There is a high correlation between one's spirituality and healing for the whole person, including the physical dimension. All this is to say:

The deeper the spiritual life of a person, the greater that person's ability to cope with the issues of living that would steal away the joy of feeling good.

We are just beginning to accumulate data to support this observation. However, those of us who have ministered in clinical settings for a quarter century and more know firsthand through professional experiences that people with strong spiritual values seem to come through illness, injuries, and surgeries more successfully than those who appear to be without such resources (or perhaps more correctly, have not tapped into the spiritual resources available to them).

Many doctors know this and consequently encourage their patients to draw on their spiritual resources. A surgeon providing an in-service class for staff nurses told them, "A visit by a patient's pastor or priest the night before surgery is more effective than any medication I could prescribe."

The spiritual dimension in feeling good is in fact the root of it all. Because we have been created by God, we human beings are religious creatures. We are aware of a force, a source, or a resource that is outside, above, and beyond ourselves and yet is as close and intimate as our very own breath. The experience of living teaches us that we cannot go it alone and still feel good about life. We need to draw on that force, that power which is the Spirit of God within us.

The Continuum of Spirituality

Some people scoff at this and speak only of self-sufficiency and self-reliance. They claim "spiritual independence" and deny any need for the benefit of a power beyond themselves. Some are adamant about this; they believe they are complete unto themselves and are offended by the notion that they should even need a higher power. They refer to the spiritual dimension as fantasy or an opiate. "I don't need any God. I can do it myself." The need for strength or support from a supernatural power flies in the face of their "bootstrap" philosophy.

At the other extreme of the continuum of spirituality is the position held by fanatics. Fanatics are usually highly prejudiced and harshly judgmental. They have an unhealthy and unbiblical dependence on faith that is expressed in statements such as, "I am completely helpless in this situation—there is nothing I can do about it; it is all in God's hands," "God will take care of it," "If God wants it to be, it will be," "This experience in which I find myself can only be resolved by God—I am powerless."

Finding our midpoint on the continuum of spirituality involves respecting our dependence on the power and support of God and denying absolute self-reliance. Part of the process of maturing is realizing that we cannot always do all things by ourselves. Depending on a power beyond ourselves gives us a realistic confidence for living, developing, and enjoying life. We depend on the multitude of resources available to us to enhance our spirituality (prayer, meditation, worship, etc.). But we still make responsible choices. We act! By actively risking and investing ourselves in living, we bear the consequences of our actions and shape our destinies. We rely on God, but we use the gifts that God has given us.

Much like developing children, we move in and out of dependence all our lives. Little children are most obvious in this oscillation. When learning to walk they enjoy the independence of making it on their own. But if a crowd moves in, they will quickly grab for mama's or daddy's hand. They will independently tease the cat, but if Tabby raises a fuss, they will hightail it to a source of comfort and protection.

In a sense we never grow out of this maneuver. I know that I am a force, a source, and a resource within myself alone. I have a measure of strength, power, choice, intelligence, and ability. Then again, I know that I have a greater force, source, and resource beyond myself which is nevertheless very close to me, and from which I can draw daily.

As with children, dependence on a source beyond myself enhances, encourages, and supports self-reliance. I function well through my daily rounds and perform responsibly. But I also go into the hospital chapel to meditate and pray. I quietly implore God to grant me wisdom and insight for the decision I must soon make. I leave the chapel confident that I will have the courage to decide. My dependence on God has enhanced my confidence in myself.

Three Attributes of Trust

(1) The power of trust. Faith allows us the opportunity to trust God—the force, source, resource, and power above and beyond ourselves. As with the little child, faith allows us to know that we can reach for the hand of God when "a crowd moves in" and threatens our independent walking. That's trust. As with the little child, faith allows us to know that we can scamper off to a source of comfort and protection if "Tabby raises a fuss." That's trust.

The stress level of living appears to be higher than ever before. In addition to the specific, personal concerns—the fears and worries each of us bears—think about the impact of what we can call *existential anxiety.* Existential anxiety is the result of simply being alive and functioning in society. Over each of our heads hang numerous issues that are potentially powerful threats (whether we are consciously aware of them or not). They seriously raise the stress of living and generate anxiety within us.

Simply knowing we live under the potential of nuclear annihilation can create substantial anxiety. The same is true of world conditions, especially terrorist activity. Is it safe to travel? How secure is my job? What are the possible ramifications of the seeming deterioration of the family (half our homes are one-parent homes)? What will my health be? Will my children grow up to be OK? How will I care for my aging parents? What about my future? my end?

Fear, anxiety, and the stress that results have become major problems in today's society. They grind away at and seek to wear down our joy until physical or mental illness is ultimately the result. This means that we must go beyond our own resources to find a power greater than ourselves that will protect us from becoming bound up in knots by stress and anxiety and will support us through the living of our days. *Trust in God is that power.*

(2) The riskiness of trust. I suspect that the people who lived in the first half of the first century did not experience the stress and anxiety that is rampant among those of us who live perched on the brink of the 21st century. Nevertheless, they must have had their share of concerns, because Jesus and Paul both found it fitting to address the issue. Sitting one day with a group on a gentle hillside, Jesus said:

> I tell you, do not worry about your life, what you will eat or drink; or about your body, what you will wear. Is not life more important than food, and the body more important than clothes? Look at the birds of the air; they do not sow or reap or store away in barns, and yet your heavenly Father feeds them. Are you not much more valuable than they? Who of you by worrying can add a single hour to his life?
>
> And why do you worry about clothes? See how the lilies of the field grow. They do not labor or spin. Yet I tell you that not even Solomon in all his splendor was dressed like one of these. If that is how God clothes the grass of the field, which is here today and tomorrow is thrown into the fire, will he not much more clothe

you, O you of little faith? So do not worry, saying,
"What shall we eat?" or "What shall we drink?" or
"What shall we wear?" For the pagans run after all
these things, and your heavenly Father knows that you
need them. But seek first his kingdom and his righteousness, and all these things will be given to you as
well. Therefore do not worry about tomorrow, for tomorrow will worry about itself. Each day has enough
trouble of its own (Matt. 6:25-34).

This certainly sounds spiritual, but it also seems
awfully risky. It reminds me of an exercise that was
especially popular during the encounter group days of
the late '60s and early '70s. It was called the "trust
fall." Someone would stand about three feet or so behind you. You would place your hands flatly on your
hips, stiffen your body tightly, and fall backward,
trusting that your partner would catch you in the arm-
pits a couple feet from the floor and gently lower you
down the rest of the way.

The "trust fall" was aptly named. You had to trust
that your partner would catch you, or you wouldn't
dare do it. But if you *did* trust him or her, the experience was exhilarating. It was a free fall, starting out
slowly and gaining velocity as you dropped backward,
waiting for the comforting jolt as your partner caught
you and then lowered you to the floor.

It *is* risky to act on Jesus' words. But certainly it is
no more risky than carrying around a load of anxiety
and a burden of stress. I have a friend whose job was
recently threatened. Funding was withdrawn for much
of what he did. I knew it frightened him, but I also
knew that he trusted that the ultimate outcome would
be favorable. I know that is true because he told me

three of his dreams. All three indicated his unconscious belief in a positive outcome. My friend risked trusting; he also proceeded as though the outcome would be as he preferred it to be. Ultimately, it was.

My friend is a realist. He is not one to look potential tragedy in the face and say, "Not to worry; God will provide," and go blithely on his way. Nor did he panic and go into a state of hysteria, overwhelmed with fear and dysfunctional. He knew clearly the severity of the threat to his security. But in his faith, he risked, he trusted—God and himself.

(3) The serenity of trust. Paul gave some very sound guidelines to Christian people in the city of Philippi more than 1900 years ago. I paraphrase the words from his letter to those Philippians, Chapter 4, verses 6 and 7: "Don't worry about anything; instead pray to God about everything. Tell God all your needs; but do not fail to thank him for all his answers. When you do this you will feel the *peace* of God which is far more amazing than your human mind can comprehend. As you trust in Christ Jesus, God's peace will keep your whole being quiet and restful."

Martha told me that she and her husband had just installed (at considerable expense) a security system in their home. It protected them from intrusion, warned of smoke, fire, or lowered temperature caused by a furnace failure, provided virtually immediate assistance in the event of emergency, and brought medical care at the touch of a button. "That must help you feel very safe," I said. "Oh yes," she replied. "It's great security and gives me tremendous peace of mind."

Peace of mind is an intangible that we all need. Paul said it is ours for the taking if we trust God. He should know; he certainly faced enough stress in his life. While there may be tremendous turmoil on the surface, there can be calm beneath in the depths. It is in this *serenity* that we find the *power* of trust.

The Serenity Prayer[6]

God grant us the serenity to accept the things we cannot change, the courage to change the things we can and the wisdom to know the difference.

We Practice Our Faith by Using Our Spiritual Resources

The Serenity Prayer is a marvelous illustration of a spiritual resource. It is a tremendous support to all of us who recognize our dependence on God.

Prayer is just one resource. There are also a great many more. What follows is a partial list of resources available to us.

Twelve Spiritual Resources

(1) Prayer. Some people wonder about the efficacy of prayer. Does it really *work*? Aren't you just talking to yourself? Not long ago I saw a roadside billboard that advertised roadside billboards. It said, *"If this sign doesn't work, how come you're reading it?"*

If there is no power in prayer, why do so many people pray? If prayer is only talking to yourself, why do so many people talk to themselves?

Prayer is a privilege granted to everyone who believes in God. It is one of the greatest gifts God gives us—the opportunity to converse with the Creator. Prayer has a distinctly conversational element about it. Conversation can take place virtually anywhere, at any time. I pray a lot while I am driving to work in the morning. (No, it isn't to stay unscathed amidst the volume of vehicles on the bustling freeway.) A long time ago I discovered that those 35 minutes of driving each morning offered me the opportunity of either (1) tensing up, elevating my blood pressure and increasing my heart rate, knotting up my stomach and competing, or (2) conversing with God, sharing my concerns, opening myself to God's input and directives, and experiencing a relaxed sense of peace.

I consider myself very fortunate that I was taught and encouraged to pray at a young age. Prayer is the greatest spiritual resource we have. In prayer we express the heights of our joy and the depths of our sadness, the profane and the profound, agony and ecstasy, longing and gratitude, humor and anger, exasperation, depression, frustration, and love—and God listens.

Prayer does not offer the one who prays any guarantee of quick fixes or solutions to the manifold issues in our lives. But it does provide us with a stabilizer and perhaps even a rudder for our journey through the turbulence of life.

(2) Meditation. I am often tempted to treat prayer and meditation together as one resource. Meditation may indeed involve prayer, and prayer can be a form of mini-meditation; but actually they are separate, largely because of the element of time and the difference in the psychic depth of prayer and meditation.

Meditation is as old as humanity's experience of the spiritual dimension of life. Meditative exercises have traditionally endeavored to free persons from the many distractions of daily life in order to become more attuned to the presence of God. The expectation of meditation has been that through this process one would experience the refreshing, supportive, calming power of God in one's own being. One would then rise from meditation feeling empowered by God's Spirit.

There appears to be a renewed interest in meditation in the midst of today's society. No doubt this is due to an increasing awareness that our preoccupation with the outer world, largely through mechanization and technologization, has cost us dearly in terms of our relationship with the inner world, and we had jolly well better do something about it. Because of this great interest, a flood of meditative materials, modes, and methods has hit the marketplace.

The beauty of meditation is that it is simple and free. Essentially all historic methods of meditation can be reduced to the employment of four simple elements and the personal development of a technique to employ the elements. The four elements are:

(a) a quiet environment.
(b) a mental device or an object on which to focus your attention.
(c) a passive attitude.
(d) a comfortable position.

(a) A quiet environment. The first element necessary is a quiet, calm place—a room, place of worship, or out of doors—where you can turn off internal stimuli as well as the possibility of external distractions.

(b) A mental device or an object on which to focus your attention. To turn off the mind's inclination toward logical, externally oriented thought, you need a

constant stimulus: fixed gazing at an object, concentration on a particular feeling, or repeating a sound, word, or phrase silently or aloud. One of the most obvious threats to meditation is "mind-wandering." The repetition of the sound or the gaze at the object helps discourage the intrusion of distracting thoughts. It is helpful also to give attention to your normal breathing pattern and let it enhance the repetition of the sound or the fixation of your gaze.

(c) A passive attitude. Forget about performance; that is, do not be concerned about how well you are doing or not doing. Because this element is of extreme importance in meditation, adopt a "let it happen" attitude. Distracting thoughts will occur; images and feelings will drift into your awareness. Do not concentrate on them but simply allow them to pass on by redirecting your attention to your repetition or gaze. Do not worry about the intrusion. Do not fear that you are not "doing it right."

(d) A comfortable position. Assume a position that will allow you to remain that way for 20 minutes. You may kneel, sit, or lie down. (However, if you lie down, there is the tendency to fall asleep.) Let your posture be such that there is no undue muscular tension.

A few years ago, Herbert Benson with Miriam Z. Klipper wrote a small book entitled, *The Relaxation Response* (Avon, 1976), in which they contrasted the practice of meditation with the stress of current living and noted the great benefits of this spiritual resource. I like their approach because of its simplicity and because they have demonstrated that practicing this technique for 10 to 20 minutes, once or twice daily, can greatly enhance personal well-being. Their technique is essentially this:[7]

(a) Assume a comfortable position in a quiet place.
(b) Close your eyes. (Benson and Klipper's technique is to use sound rather than gaze as the mental device.)
(c) Relax all your muscles by beginning at your feet and progressing up to your face. Remain so relaxed.
(d) Breathe through your nose and become aware of your breathing. As you breathe out, say the word *one* (or some other sound or word) silently to yourself. Breathe easily and naturally.
    (1) Breathe in.
    (2) Breathe out.
    (3) Say to yourself, "one."
    (4) Breathe in.
    (5) Breathe out.
    (6) Say to yourself, "one."
    (7) Etc.
(e) Continue for 10 to 20 minutes. Open your eyes to check the time if your wish, but do not use an alarm. When you have finished, sit quietly for several minutes, first with your eyes closed, and then with them open. Do not stand up.
(f) Maintain a passive attitude throughout and permit relaxation to occur at its own pace. When distracting thoughts enter, do not dwell on them but return to repeating your sound.

(3) Reading the Bible. Whether one reads Scripture randomly or follows a systematic pattern or program, the experience of Bible reading is an excellent spiritual resource. Bible stories, the four Gospels, and Paul's

letters are particularly helpful. No matter how often I have read a passage, it seems that something I had not seen before presents itself to me in another reading.

(4) Reading devotional literature. There is an amazing wealth of helpful devotional literature available today. Inspirational biographies and stories from people's lives abound. Daily devotional literature is available in a wide variety of booklet forms. New books are continually produced to provide devotional literature for different age groups, ranging from small children to the elderly, for men and women, couples and singles, parents and children. Material is available relating to the seasons of life and various special topics.

Reading devotional literature in conjunction with reading the Bible is very supportive. We feel the sense of unity with others in the literature—identification and empathy. We experience a feeling of "belonging" in the household of God. Devotional literature and Bible reading can help us clarify issues we struggle with, uplift us in troubled times, and help solidify our identity in the communion of saints.

Perusing the catalog of materials available from religious publishing houses or browsing through a religious bookstore will provide anyone with a multitude of opportunities to make use of these resources.

(5) Participation in worship. This resource, also, gives us the experience of "belonging." Worship reminds us we are not alone—we are a part of the fellowship of believers, the communion of saints. Worship is supportive and renewing. It combines many spiritual resources: Bible reading, religious music, art, and literature. Worship reminds us of God's forgiveness through the Lord's Supper. But worship may also

be informal, as well as formal, and solitary as well as corporate.

(6) Listening to religious music. We all have our favorites, don't we? Mine are Handel's *Messiah,* Bach's *Mass in B Minor,* and Brahms' *Requiem.* In its own way, each of these masterpieces can virtually catapult me into a wonderful sense of God's closeness. Consider also the power, reverence, and compassion of great hymns. I think of Isaac Watts' great hymn fashioned out of Psalm 90:

> *O God, our help in ages past,*
> *Our hope for years to come,*
> *Be thou our guide while troubles last,*
> *And our eternal home!*

Every time I sing the magnificent "Praise to the Lord, the Almighty, the King of Creation," my spirit soars. I sing the words, "Ponder anew what the Almighty can do," and my doubts and fears fade as I say to myself, "Oh yes, don't forget—nothing is impossible for God."

Probably one of the most moving of all hymns is the great spiritual, "Were You There When They Crucified My Lord?" You cannot hear or sing those words without feeling the compassion and love that God has for us. You walk away from that hymn convinced that the love and compassion manifested through Jesus Christ will never fail you.

(7) Viewing religious art. A great many people have been gifted with the talent to speak to our spirits through their art—sculpture, painting, stained glass, and architecture. All these vehicles have the ability to

fortify our faith. Next time you encounter religious art, take time to let it give you its message.

(8) Taking a sabbath rest. Let your "seventh day" be qualitatively different from your other six. Find a different environment in which to enjoy it. If you work at a desk or at a machine, travel. If you travel, "stay put" and spend time at a hobby. If you work in isolation, get out among people. If you are surrounded by people in your work, isolate yourself with just your family around. Use the spiritual resource of a sabbath rest to change your pace and refresh your spirit.

(9) Participation in church and charitable activities. Do things for others! Not only will others benefit, so will you. Refer back to Key Number 3.

(10) Participation in spiritual retreats. Retreats provide an excellent opportunity to recharge your spiritual batteries. They can provide you with a vital sense of renewal for the practice of your faith and the joy of feeling good.

(11) Fasting. Fasting as a spiritual resource provides you with a *heightening of your awareness of your spiritual dimension*. Fasting can also help you gain the experience of hunger, and thus identify with the situation of two-thirds of the world's population. (But since fasting can also be dangerous to the health of some persons, or for anyone without proper guidance, check with your medical professional before you begin. A well-known guide to spiritual fasting is *God's Chosen Fast* by Arthur Wallis [Christian Literature Crusade, 1970.])

(12) Conversation with a fellow traveler. A fellow traveler is any other person who sees life as, among

other things, a spiritual pilgrimage. Many people have found it supportive and beneficial to share experiences of their spiritual journeys with another trusted person. This can also take place within a small group (of no more than five or six) of fellow travelers. Sharing insights, experiences, and the bearing of burdens is an effective method for spiritual growth and enrichment.

Three More Resources

Beyond the dozen resources listed above there are three more that can help keep us on a path between spiritual overdependence and independence. These are somewhat different than the others and need to be considered separately.

(1) Doubt. Doubt is most definitely a spiritual resource. Doubt is a normal aspect of faith that helps faith to increase. Doubt asks the questions that pushes faith into new arenas. Doubt stretches and expands faith.

Some people have the idea that faith never doubts. "Not *true* faith," they say. Don't believe them. It simply isn't true. To chart the movement of faith is not to draw a straight line beginning down in the lower left corner of the chart and proceeding ever onward, ever upward without interruption. That is idealism, not realism. A more accurate diagram of faith's movement would look something like a year's charting of the daily Dow Jones Industrial Average.

When you experience doubt in your faith, identify it, accept it, and talk it out with a fellow traveler. Do not keep it to yourself. A doubt can be an obstacle to faith *only if you deny it and suppress it*. Together with your fellow traveler, use the many spiritual resources available to bring the doubt to resolution. Remember, God is faithful, even when we are faithless. That is the bottom line.

(2) Forgiveness. Guilt is one of the greatest foes of the joy of feeling good. Forgiveness, the antidote to guilt, is one of joy's greatest friends. "Though your sins are like scarlet, they shall be as white as snow," said God (Isa. 1:18). And again, "As far as the east is from the west, so far has he removed our transgressions from us" (Ps. 103:12).

Guilt is the consequence of sin—that is very clear. But "if we confess our sins, he is faithful and just and will forgive us our sins and purify us from all unrighteousness" (1 John 1:9). That is what Good Friday and Easter are all about. "For God so loved the world that he gave his one and only Son, that whoever believes in him shall not perish but have eternal life" (John 3:16).

Accept God's forgiveness and forgive yourself. Do not say you accept God's forgiveness and then continue to hold onto your guilt. That is egotism and will only generate stress within you. If you find it difficult to accept God's forgiveness or to forgive yourself, share your trouble with a fellow traveler, that together you may come to the full benefit of the spiritual resource of forgiveness.

(3) Hope. Hope is the power of positive expectation. Hope also heightens our ability to fight disease, while depression lowers it.

Change—even traumatic change—always brings with it the opportunity for spiritual growth. It is vital that those who suffer not lose sight of hope. Hope may sometimes appear to be obliterated by powerful feelings of despair and anger. Yet it is never completely crushed, but rises up again and again, ultimately to bloom—if not in this life, then in the next.

All Things Are Relative

From time to time, discouragement takes a front-row seat in our lives and the flame of faith burns dimly. We wonder just how it is all going to turn out. There is not one among us who has not experienced that. But then God, who "moves in mysterious ways his wonders to perform," enters the scene and reminds us of what we have temporarily forgotten—God *is*!

When I first heard Peter Niewiek tell his story, my skin turned to gooseflesh and I was overwhelmed. Never in my life had I had the significance of relativity driven home so profoundly; particularly as it relates to strength and weakness.

Peter said: "Things are not always what they seem to be. When my wife, Mary and I reflect on this spiritual principle, we are reminded of a hike we took with another couple around a mountain lake. The hike had been tiring for me and somewhat painful. Just two months earlier physicians had found large malignant tumors in my body. My life was in jeopardy. The effects of the disease and the treatment made the hike difficult, but the emotional effects of all of this made it seem important to get out and enjoy each other, loving friends, and the beauty of the scenery.

"As we stood on the far side of the lake and looked back at the mountain, our friend Myrna asked, 'What's the matter? Is something wrong?'

"The walk around the lake had lifted my spirit considerably. A slight breeze raised small, friendly-looking waves that made sparkling play with the sun's rays. Dark-green fir trees spired more than a hundred feet into the cloudless sky. A dominant, snowcapped peak stood sentinel as background to the scene. The couple we were with was easy to respect and like.

"As we reached the far side of the lake, we discovered a rustic lodge hidden in the trees at the foot of a waterfall. It was situated so lodgers could have the best view of the lake and mountain. It could be reached only by water or by a hiking trail. It was special.

"Mary inquired about reservations. She thought it would be a fine place for a restful family vacation. Upon learning that the nearest open time was one year from the present week, she talked with the manager about reserving that time. The rest of us wandered toward the shore.

"Myrna asked me again, 'What's troubling you?' This time I replied, 'The mountain, the lake, the trees—they all seem to be based on the very foundations of the earth. Because of this disease, my life seems to be hanging from a hair. Mary is in there making reservations for next year. I may not even be here, *alive*, next year.'

"I had not forgotten that God cares and that the church was praying for my recovery. But that all seemed quite airy next to the solidness of the scene before me.

"We never did get to use our reservations that next summer. *I* was here, but Harmony Falls Lodge was gone. So was the lake. The fir trees were gone too. Even the mountain was gone, at least in its centuries-old form. Mount St. Helens had blown away Spirit Lake, Harmony Falls Lodge, and literally everything!

"It still seems odd," concluded Peter, "at times even funny. What seemed so solid and strong is gone. What seemed so shaky and weak remains."

"Faith is being sure of what we hope for and certain of what we do not see." So said the writer of the New Testament letter to the Hebrews (11:1). Faith is powerful, because its source is the Spirit of God within us. Because of faith, you and I can be sure of what we hope for and certain of what we cannot see. That provides us with realistic confidence—confidence that we have spiritual resources at our disposal.

Practice *your* faith, and experience the joy of feeling good!

Live Your Own Life

Finding your path between powerlessness and omnipotence.

*J*oe stared vacantly at the door in my office. His spouse, Julia, sat across from him dabbing at her eyes with a tissue. We had come to the point of facing head-on Joe's division of love between his wife and his work. As an upwardly-moving building contractor, Joe felt the need to be on top of everything in his company. Many times he had said to me privately, "I have to know everything that is going on. We are talking about millions of dollars moving around here. One mistake and I could lose my shirt."

He had presented an impressive case; so impressive that Julia "bought it" for many years. Recently, however, she had begun to point out to him that his dedication to the development of his company was displacing his dedication to his wife and children. There was no question of his love for them, but it seemed to pale in comparison to his love for his business. "You are hardly ever home; and when you are, you're irritable. You lie to me, telling me you are going to drive around to relax or go to the health club to work out, when actually you go to your office and work! It's like you are having an affair—only not with a woman—with your desk!''

Joe began to make a feeble attempt to rationalize and justify his behavior. As he continued, he became more and more animated, working himself up, speaking faster and snappier. He reached inside his jacket and produced a pocket date book. He leafed through the pages, poked at a page with his finger, and barked, "Look! Look at this! What am I supposed to do? Meeting here at 8:00; meeting there at 10:00. Inspect this, go to that. Be here, be there. If I don't do all these things I'm in real trouble. Don't you understand? I can't do anything about this! What am I supposed to do?''

As Joe had talked, I had become increasingly excited too. My empathy was running full throttle. I entered into the discussion right at his pitch. I grabbed his right arm and said, "Listen! Listen to me, Joe. I *know* what you're talking about. I know the feeling." I released his arm, spun around in my swivel chair, snatched my "Day at a Glance" appointment book from my desk top, turned back to him, and began flapping the book in front of him.

My voice was intense; I punched out the words. "You see this? This book? You know what this is? This is my appointment book—just like yours; only *bigger*! I used to say the same things that you say. I used to moan and complain. I *hated* the book. 'This book is living my *life* for me' I would say.''

Joe's eyes were wide. He was on the edge of his chair, nodding, head bobbing, yes, that's it, Bill, that's just the way it is. My emotion was as intense as his. Still waving the appointment book, I exclaimed, "Then . . . one . . . day, sitting in this chair . . . it *dawned* on me. It struck me broadside; and I laughed. I just threw myself back in this chair and I howled. 'You fool,' I said. 'You poor, simple fool!' Then, hammering each word with a slap of the book on the palm of my left hand, I shouted, *'You're . . . the one . . . who writes . . . in . . . the book!' "*

Silence. There was absolute silence. We needed time to come down from the intensity. Finally, Joe spoke. "You're right," he said quietly. "I'm the one who writes in my book, too. I'm in charge; or I *can* be in charge of what goes in it."

The three of us set out on the journey of restructuring a life. Ultimately Joe chose to let go of his need to be on top of all aspects of his business. He engaged a consultant who helped him reorganize his staff so that he could entrust responsibilities to others. In time, Joe became able to deal with his compulsion to work, achieve, and acquire, realizing how much of it came from his low self-esteem. Leaving that behind, he moved on to live his own life.

Joe's story is helpful because, in a sense, he presented himself at both extremes of this continuum. On the one hand, he appeared to be at the extreme of omnipotence and almightiness, apparently saying, "I can do everything." Then again he presented himself at the other extreme, as powerless and impotent, saying, "I can't do anything about this! What am I supposed to do?" Joe could not feel good about his life at either extreme. It was only through discovering his

own path to a midpoint between them that he was able
to live his life with a satisfactory degree of fulfillment
and happiness, and know the joy of feeling good.

Why do people find themselves at the extremes?
What are the reasons for the attitudes of *powerlessness*
and *omnipotence?* There appear to be several reasons
for each one.

Some Reasons for the Extreme of Powerlessness

(1) Fear of the unknown. People who present themselves at the powerless end of this continuum are often
people who fear the unknown and are consequently
unwilling to risk letting go of their position. When I
first met Ellen, she was, by her own calculation, 45
pounds overweight. She had been in four different
structured weight loss programs, and had left each of
them without success. She was distressed because she
wanted very much to enter into an intimate and meaningful relationship with a man, become married, and
begin a home and family. She was 29 years old, and
she had never had a close relationship with a male
person. She attributed this to "their lack of interest in
my excess pounds."

In our conversations together it became clear that
Ellen's fear of the unknown kept her powerless to live
her own life. She really *did* want to achieve what she
said she wanted. But on the other hand the very thought
of it created anxiety within her. Close relationships
with boys, young men, and men had never yet been a
part of her experience. This was uncharted territory;
desirable but terrifying. Suppose she *were* to begin to

develop a relationship with a man. What would she do? Would she frighten him off? Or suppose the relationship got off the ground, but then he rejected her?

As she had grown older in years she had intuitively learned that the best way to protect herself against possible rejection was not to risk a relationship. Early on she discovered that being overweight was an almost sure-fire disqualifier to entering boy-girl relationships. So her poor body image (supported by a poor self-image) had succeeded in protecting her from the risks (and rewards) that come with an intimate relationship with someone of the opposite sex.

(2) Reluctance to "change the record." Many people choose to continue to believe things that they find out are not true. They "know better," but they simply do not change. Parental messages often ascribe powerlessness to a developing young person. "Don't think you're so smart. You're not smart at all." "You'll never amount to anything; you're all thumbs." "You can't do *anything* right, can you?" The power of parental influence is so great that it may continue from beyond the grave. So the record keeps playing, and the child (now an adult) is reluctant to change the record.

To "change the record" requires discipline and work. We all know that old ruts are hard to get out of. Getting caught in a rut while driving requires a substantial cut of the wheel to jump the vehicle out of it, and then you run the risk of possibly losing control. Changing old patterns is not only frightening, but often undesirable. Besides, everyone knows that while old shoes may be shabby, they're certainly very comfortable.

(3) Refusal of responsibility. "My life is simply a fallen leaf tossed about by the October winds." That is a rather dramatic and poetic way of phrasing this third reason for a feeling of powerlessness—refusal of responsibility. This refusal involves projecting personal responsibility onto anything or anyone other than oneself. "If it weren't for our family's poverty, I could have attended the university." "If you hadn't distracted me, I wouldn't have backed the car into the garage." "Now look what you made me do." "If my lover hadn't deserted me, I wouldn't have overdosed."

People who believe that their lives are controlled and shaped by outside forces will not accept responsibility for what they do. Abandoning personal responsibility for this reason may appear to take one "off the hook," but it also leaves one powerless to live one's own life.

Some Reasons for the Extreme of Omnipotence

(1) Anger and vengence. There is a hostile kind of omnipotence that appears to be motivated by the desire to settle a score. It may be overt or covert. It is a result of deciding that life has handed a person a bad deal and he or she is going to show *them.* "I'll get even. Life cannot dump on me and get away with it."

Often the root of this position is the person's having overcome a great obstacle or setting out to overcome one. Horatio Alger-type persons, who have overcome the degradation of poverty by pulling themselves up by their bootstraps, may present themselves at this end of the continuum. So may persons who become successful by stepping on others. Sometimes such persons present a congenial persona, but beneath it their philosophy is, "Get them before they get you."

(2) Grandiosity. People may appear at the "nothing-I-cannot-do" end of this continuum because of an inflated sense of self. This is a perfectionistic attitude, fueled by lack of trust and need for control. The attitude is characterized by statements such as, "I am the only one who can do this." "If I can't do it, it won't be done." "If I don't do it, it won't be done right."

There is generally a background of insecurity behind this position and this is what generates the lack of trust and need for control. Incidentally, both extremes on this continuum are clearly seen in this dimension of control. Those at one extreme believe they can control everything. Those at the opposite extreme believe they are controlled *by* everything.

(3) Messiahship. One may develop messiahship (see Key Number 3) through a willingness or need to take on more and more responsibility. This may come from old guilt (I have to make up for what I did in the past), an overbearing need to be accepted and liked by everyone (I will do "anything for anyone"), a generally shaky self-image (I need to demonstrate my value by doing and doing because performance equals value), or the belief that this truly is one's calling in life.

This last factor is a highly exaggerated form of the philosophy of most people in the helping professions. People enter these professions because they want to help others. However, often the needs of the people being helped outdistance the resources of the helping professional. If the need to be needed is sufficiently great, messiahship will be the consequence, and burnout will be the tangible result.

Here is one of the places where living on the extreme of a continuum clearly demonstrates its damaging effects. Psychologist Christine Maslach defines burnout as "a state of physical, emotional and mental exhaustion marked by physical depletion and chronic fatigue, feelings of helplessness and hopelessness, and by development of negative self-concept and negative attitudes towards work, life and other people."[8]

The signs of burnout include:

- decreased energy to perform.
- feelings of failure in vocation.
- a reduced sense of reward for having put so much of one's self into the work.
- a sense of helplessness and inability to see a way out of problems.
- cynicism and negativism about self, others, work, and the world in general.

Either extreme on this continuum can destroy the joy of feeling good. Instead, seek out your path between the two extremes and *live your own life*. No doubt you've heard people say, "I'd rather burn out than rust out." Fortunately, those are not the only two alternatives. The following are several suggestions to help you locate your midpoint.

Eight Ways to Help You Live Your Own Life

(1) Exercise your power of choice. God in his wisdom has seen fit to endow us human beings with free choice over earthly affairs. As we go about our lives

we are free to choose between alternatives. Choices always exist. Some people want to refute that statement, because sometimes the choices that are available are not very attractive. While we may be blessed with having to choose between good, better, and best, or between good and evil, often we also are faced with choosing between bad, worse, and worst. And when all the alternatives are undesirable, we are tempted to say, "I have no choice."

Sound decision making helps you live your own life. But you can't make a sound decision unless you know the array of choices you have. Get in the habit of listing (on paper) *all* the alternatives you can think of as you face an issue that needs resolution. As I counsel with people I find that much of my work is helping them hold up to themselves options that they would not consider to be options. Therefore I suggest that you seek diligently to include *all* possible choices in the issues you face. This will help prevent you from sliding into the temptation to give away your power and say, "I can't do anything about it. I simply don't have a choice." Don't paralyze your resources with unnecessary extra stress by feeling locked into an unalterable situation.

Often people will choose to act on an alternative that initially appeared to be highly undesirable, but which turned out to be not so bad after all. Then they are heard to say something like, "Why didn't I do that long ago?"

Stop projecting and take responsibility. Each of us has the choice of either taking personal responsibility for our behavior or projecting that responsibility elsewhere. The great temptation, of course, is to project it elsewhere, because then we can enjoy the goodies of freedom without the resultant responsibilities. This may seem attractive, but it will cost us dearly in terms of personal integrity and personal power.

Assuming responsibility for our behavior takes courage, but it pays off in personal integrity and feeling good about oneself. When you choose to say, "Yes, you're right; that was not a wise decision on my part, I should have given more consideration to other possibilities," instead of, "Don't blame me. I couldn't do a thing about it," you begin to live your own life.

You *can* more than you *can't;* and you don't *have* to as much as you *think* you have to.

Most of the time when we say, "I can't," what we actually mean is, "I could if I wanted to, but I don't want to." Most of the time when we say, "I have to," we really mean, "I don't want to, but I'm going to."

We limit our power of choice and free will by habitually using "can't" and "have to." By admitting at least to ourselves that we "don't want to" rather than "can't," and we "choose to" rather than "have to," we build our integrity by not trying to fool ourselves. The "I have tos" can push you into the burnout of messiahship, and the "I can'ts" can keep you chained to impotence.

What if George Washington, buried in the snows of Valley Forge, had said, "I can't"?

What if Franklin D. Roosevelt, struck down with infantile paralysis, had said, "I can't"?

What if Glenn Cunningham, who at age 3 was burned so severely in a schoolhouse fire that doctors said he would never walk again, had said, "I can't"?

(In 1934 Cunningham set the world's record for the mile: 4 minutes, 6.8 seconds.)

What if Martin Luther King Jr., born black in a society filled with racial discrimination, had said, "I can't"?

What if Madame Curie, who was told, "Science is not for women," had said, "I can't"?

What if Max Cleland, who lost both legs and an arm in Vietnam, had said, "I can't"? (Cleland became head of the Veteran's Administration.)

What if Grandma Moses, who at age 80 was told she was too old to start painting, had said, "I can't"?

What if Toscanini, second fiddle in an obscure South American orchestra, had said, "I can't"?

What if John Milton, blind at age 44, had said, "I can't"? (Sixteen years later Milton wrote *Paradise Lost*.)

(2) Be able to say yes and no to yourself and to others. That impressive list above speaks admirably to being able to say yes as you live your own life.

Saying no is just as important, for this is what prevents us from running headlong into omnipotence or messiahship. Do you remember Joe from the beginning of this chapter? Joe didn't know how to say no to himself, so he wondered, "Am I living my own life or is my life being lived for me?" When he began to limit his "yeses" and exercise his "nos," he found his own midpoint on the continuum.

You can avoid burnout. *You do not have to burn out.* Remember that we *do* have a choice—we *always* have a choice. Avoid taking on more than you can physically and mentally handle. If you refuse to do this, you may very well find an unconscious escape from your escalating burden of responsibility by falling ill. In our society illness is much more acceptable than refusal. For instance, if you ask me to do more and more, and I refuse, you may be offended. But if you ask me to do more and more and I become ill, that will be acceptable.

How to say no to other people (without feeling guilty). It is easy to believe that we have a certain obligation to do what other people ask us to, whether we want to or not. If that is our belief, then to say no will, of course, generate guilt. "I really should do it (even though I don't want to). After all, it's only polite." We may also fear that we will let the other person down. "After all, they're obviously counting on me. I really should say yes."

"Honesty is the best policy." That is as true in this as in anything else. If you know that you do not want to do what is being asked of you, politely say, "Thank you, but I don't want to do that." Actually you have no obligation to go beyond that response in terms of explanation or reasons. Being polite in your response adequately fulfills your responsibility.

A task force on which I had served for about a year was finally completing its business and had decided to go ahead with its project. This decision involved the securing of funds from outside the organization to get the project off the ground. The chairperson of the task force said, "Finding outside funding will involve writing grant proposals to foundations who would be interested in our project." Motioning to the woman on his right, he continued, "Louise, our P.R. person, has agreed to go to work on this." Then looking at me he said, "Bill, will you help her do the writing? You certainly write well."

I quickly reviewed what he had said and what I knew would be involved, and I slowly replied, "No, I don't want to do that, John. I've extended myself as far as I want to be extended at this time, and I don't want to take on any more responsibilities. Thank you, though, for your compliment and your confidence."

An honest, straightforward, and simple answer will usually settle the issue. In this case I didn't have to feel any guilt, and in fact I didn't.

You may feel a need to embellish your *no* more than that. Note the strategies that are used in this illustration provided by psychologist Barry Lubetkin: "While Loretta was at a co-op board meeting, the president asked her to serve as head of the decoration committee. Despite her initial impulse to say 'yes,' she stalled: 'It sounds like a good idea, and I'm sure I could do the job. But I have a few other obligations, and I need a day to think about it.' A day later, Loretta called the president back and told him she was flattered that he wanted her for the job but that she just didn't have the time. He then attempted to pressure her by saying, 'There's no one else who could do it as well as you.' She came back with, 'As a matter of fact, you're so artistic, you could do an even better job than I could. If you're too busy, why don't you try Jan or Nancy? They did a bang-up job on the landscaping last year.' He then switched to guilt, pointing out that he'd done favors for her when she chaired a committee he was on. She teased him by pointing out that she thought she'd paid back that debt already, and she reminded him that she hadn't signed anything in blood. Finally he gave up good-naturedly."[9]

Assert yourself without aggressiveness. The essential difference between assertiveness and aggressiveness is that assertiveness is straightforward and arises out of positive self-image, self-esteem, and self-confidence, while aggressiveness includes more negative aspects of attack and combativeness and usually arises out of a fragile self-image, uncertainty, and self-doubt. Assertiveness based on self-confidence facilitates communication; it is authentic and respects the other person. Aggressiveness, on the other hand, may be a "big noise covering up a shaky self," and it tends to be more "pushy and shoving" of the other person, possibly raising defenses and shutting down open communication.

Caring about the other person is a significant part of assertiveness. This is helpful in being able to say no and will help make the task easier.

(3) Share responsibility. Avoid the "only I can do it" syndrome, and share your responsibilities with others. If you truly believe that everything will self-destruct if you are not available to keep it from self-destructing, you are doing something wrong.

When Joe finally risked sharing responsibility with others in his organization, he gained much more than he gave up. The division of responsibility generated a new collegiality that Joe's previous attitude had discouraged. His associates now felt they were an integral part of the organization, whereas previously they often felt like outsiders looking in. No matter how much skill and saavy Joe had about the business, his team's combined expertise far surpassed it.

Letting *go* and letting *others* is very wise.

(4) Be open to the input of others. A few years ago there was a popular song entitled, "I Did It My Way." One could interpret the lyrics as either speaking to rugged individualism or brash arrogance. Either

way, this is an issue that needs to be considered seriously.

Allow yourself to be open to other peoples' critical feedback, ideas, and suggestions. None of us is particularly fond of criticism, let alone nonconstructive criticism. But people usually do not just "make up" criticism—the criticism may be exaggerated, but there is probably a core of truth to it. Try not only to hear but to *listen* to feedback from others. Even though it is hard to hear and accept, feedback from our spouse, colleague, or close friend or relative is one of the best ways to learn about ourselves. (See Key Number 4.)

Try to avoid getting locked into your own limited ideas. Avoid the practice of some leaders who conscientiously solicit feedback and input from subordinates, but end up doing things their way, because, after all, they are the ones who "know best."

Keep a list of the feedback items you have received—the suggestions, ideas, and criticisms. Study them with an open mind, ideally with another, trusted person. As you come to new insights, integrate them into your life and celebrate your growth.

(5) Diversify. One of the elements common to both extremes of this continuum is boredom. A solution to that problem is to diversify your interests and activities. If overactivity is an issue, cancel or phase out two current involvements and replace them with one that is substantially different from what you are overloaded with. If "feeling unable" is an issue, get into a group class or project, possibly in the evening adult education program of your school district.

Seek new and different interests. If you lean toward the overextended end of this continuum, always *substitute*, do not add onto, current involvements. Develop a hobby, possibly even an avocation. Learn how to goof off and be unproductive. This latter assignment is a difficult one for many of us, particularly if, in our value system, we believe that it is wrong (or even sinful) to waste time. But nonproductivity is certainly a diversification from perpetual productivity, so try it.

(6) Talk out your issues and concerns. If you feel dissatisfied with the way you are living your life, don't keep these concerns to yourself. Share them with a trusted friend, a "fellow traveler," a counselor or a therapist. Another person's objectivity can help you see more clearly the issues you face and can also skillfully help you along your road to resolving them. Counselors do not provide magical answers. They are skilled guides who will patiently walk with you along your path.

(7) Develop and keep a sense of humor. Did your mother or anyone ever tell you when you were a youngster that you ought to wear clean underwear whenever you "went out," just in case you were in an accident and had to be taken to a hospital where the people in the emergency department would take off your clothes so they could treat you, and you wouldn't be embarrassed by dirty underwear?

We have heard so much lately about excellence. Do you suppose there is a place within excellence for dirty underwear? I hope so; otherwise a lot of us are in deep trouble.

We human beings have the gift of self-awareness. This gift helps us to be responsible beings and to take ourselves and our earthly existence seriously. Too often, though, we take ourselves far more seriously than is necessary or healthy, and we expect that of other people too. When they don't take themselves seriously, we become distressed. We are reminded that imperfection still exists, despite all our efforts to the contrary.

There *is* imperfection in life, and it continues whether we like it or not. If we accept that as a fact, then we either (1) ignore it (and become a kind of hermit), (2) get bent out of shape by it (and live unhappily ever after), or (3) find humor in it (and conclude that yes, there *is* room within excellence for dirty underwear).

If we are willing to accept our imperfection, we can accept the imperfection of others. If we refuse to take ourselves too seriously, we will be able to laugh at our foibles and shortcomings. We will be able to laugh with others as they laugh at *their* imperfections. When you are faced with a situation that tempts you to complain, see if you can find some humor in it somewhere. When you are tempted to take yourself or someone else too seriously, ask yourself the question, "One hundred years from now, will it really make any difference?" That will produce some healthy laughter.

The ability to appreciate humor and to laugh are positive signs of the joy of feeling good. Physiologically, the act of laughing is known to affect the cardiovascular, respiratory, endocrine, and nervous systems. Psychiatrist Dr. Donald W. Black, from the University of Iowa, says there is an intriguing analogy between laughing and exercise. Physically, "Laughing involves muscle contractions followed by a period of relaxation; activation of the brain, the pituitary and adrenal glands; elevation of the pulse rate; all of which occur when we engage in exercise."[10]

When Norman Cousins wrote his book, *Anatomy of an Illness As Perceived by the Patient* (Norton, 1979), he described his remarkable dealings with a crippling disease which the doctors believed to be irreversible. Cousins determined to use all of his own capabilities for overcoming illness, not the least of which was laughter. He discovered that laughter was good medicine for him. "I made the joyous discovery that 10 minutes of genuine belly laughter (from viewing "Candid Camera" and Marx Brothers films) had an anesthetic effect and would give me at least two hours of painfree sleep." Laughter had a salutary effect on his body's chemistry and enhanced his system's ability to fight his disease.

It's good advice: "Laugh a little; live a lot!"

(8) Take time to smell the flowers. As you live your own life, make sure that you take time to have fun, to play, to let the child in you romp freely, to refresh, to revitalize, and to recreate.

Fun is critical to healthy development and a sense of well-being. Research indicates that young apes who are deprived of fun and play grow up to have distorted, neurotic personalities. In this regard, the difference between people and animals is that people have many more kinds of play to enjoy, ranging from the obvious to the very subtle.

Do it! If you must, write it into your schedule. But do it. Take time to smell the flowers.

God the Creator is the giver of life to each of us. Through our talents, abilities, and freedom, we have the power of choice and the freedom to chart our destinies. More often than not, destiny does not lie out there somewhere in the unknown—destiny lies right here in our very own hands.

We *can* feel good about ourselves. We *can* celebrate the joy of feeling good. We have much more control over our lives than we like to think we do.

Note this though—however desirable it is to find your path between the extremes of each continuum, perfection is impossible. Don't expect to be perfect, and don't expect that God will love you more than he already does now. We are forgiven for our failings. We are accepted and loved as we are. And that is why we are free to use our gifts wisely and strive for balance in life.

God, the giver of life, tells us that his wish for us is that we experience a rich and full life. Jesus told us that his purpose in coming was that we might have life that is "full" (John 10:10). The Greek word for "full" could also be translated as "over and above," "more than is even necessary," "superadded," "exceedingly abundant," or "supreme." That's the kind of life that God has in mind for us. I take God to mean that that superadded, exceedingly abundant life includes the joy of feeling good. May you discover that joy!

Notes

1. The "Seven Basic Rules of Good Health" are adapted from an article by Lester Breslow and Nedra Belloc in *Preventive Medicine* 9 (1980): 469-483.
2. Thanks to Linda Stipe for this inclusive compilation.
3. From *Murder in the Cathedral* by T. S. Eliot, copyright 1935 by Harcourt Brace Jovanovich, Inc.; renewed 1963 by T. S. Eliot. Reprinted by permission of the publishers Harcourt Brace Jovanovich, Inc., and Faber and Faber.
4. Adapted from *How to Live 365 Days a Year* by John A. Schindler, M.D., copyright © 1954 by Prentice-Hall, Inc., Englewood Cliffs, N.J. Reprinted by permission of the publisher, Prentice-Hall, Inc.
5. Carl G. Jung, *Modern Man in Search of a Soul* (New York: Harcourt, Brace and Co., 1933, p. 229.
6. Originally written by Reinhold Niebuhr, The Serenity Prayer has been adopted in this form and widely used by Alcoholics Anonymous.
7. Eliciting *The Relaxation Response* from *The Relaxation Response* by Herbert Benson, M.D., with Miriam Z. Klipper, copyright © 1975 by William Morrow and Company, Inc. Adapted by permission of the author and publisher.
8. Christine Maslach, "Clergy Stress and Burnout," (Minneapolis: Ministers Life Resources), p. 3.
9. From an interview with Barry Lubetkin, "How to Say *No* without Feeling Guilty," *Bottom Line/Personal* (New York: Boardroom Reports, Inc.), February 15, 1985, p. 9.

10. Donald W. Black, M.D., in Michael Briley, "The Last Laugh! It's Good for You," *Modern Maturity*, June-July 1985, p. 30.